What people are saying about …

THE SACRED US

"Powerful, personal, and practical. *The Sacred Us* outlines and unpacks what biblical community can actually look like. Justin has created a playbook for each of us to see a whole new way of doing church. I'm fired up!"

Brad Lomenick, former president of Catalyst,
author of *H3 Leadership* and *The Catalyst Leader*

"Justin Kendrick calls us back to the biblical patterns and values that were culturally normative and spiritually formative before the advent of our modern-day mobility turned our friends and neighbors into acquaintances and HOAs. Applying his seven principles of biblical community will help you and your neighbors restore a bit of what has been so sadly lost."

Larry Osborne, pastor and author,
North Coast Church

"Never have we been more connected with less true connection. The result is that we are isolated, superficial, and lonely. *The Sacred Us* stands in stark contrast to the 'self-centered me' of our generation. Justin Kendrick paints a portrait of biblical community that is winsome, believable, and compelling. I want more of what he describes … and if we will follow Justin's road map, our lives will be more meaningful and purposeful."

Lance Witt, founder of Replenish Ministries

"When you read *Sacred Us*, you'll understand why I love Justin Kendrick. While most pastoral leaders understand the importance of building authentic community, many have a hard time actually leading people into it because they don't have it themselves. But this book has been in the making for most of Justin's life. Since his teenage years, Justin has been building the kind of genuine, multi-ethnic friendships that change people's lives for eternity. Let Justin's convictions move you to make the profound changes that turn casual, transactional church attendance into the authentic spiritual community that we all deeply long for. You will never want to just 'go to church' again!"

Dr. Darryn Scheske, senior pastor of Heartland Church, Indianapolis, chair of Converge

"If loneliness is the leprosy of the twenty-first century, *The Sacred Us* offers God's cure: radical community! Justin Kendrick's courageous call to thick friendships is exactly what the church needs post-COVID. No one wants to return to a superficial social club. But Jesus' vision of a supernatural family empowered by His Spirit is what our souls crave. If you're ready to engage the next generation of Millennials and Zoomers, don't just read *The Sacred Us*—grab your team and live it out loud!"

Tim Lucas, founder and lead pastor of Liquid Church, leadership coach at ChurchChanger.com

"This book punched me right in the gut … in the *best* way possible! It is both a sounding alarm and a wake-up call that we were not meant to do this life alone. In a time when our world is simultaneously the most accessible and yet the *loneliest* we've ever been, where we pour our hearts out to social media only to realize there is no one to check in on us the next day, we are at an epidemic, critical, crossroads moment. Enter this book as our road map and field guide pointing the way back! Pastor Justin Kendrick has been a wise, discerning, prophetic voice in my life for years as my own pastor, and I know that his is a voice that can be *trusted* with this message we all so desperately need right now. Only once in a while does a book come along that can—within just the first few pages—make you instantly sit up, take stock of your entire life, bring tears to your eyes, and give you a new, determined resolve to just do better. To go beyond these surface-level friendships and pretend community … and to truly be seen, known, and loved by other people as you show up and love them in return. *This* is that book! And I will be forever grateful to Justin for writing it. I can't wait to see all the lives that are about to be changed!"

Mary Marantz, bestselling author of *Dirt*
and *Slow Growth Equals Strong Roots,*
host of *The Mary Marantz Show*

"Justin is an advocate for transparent, generous friendships, and I am one of many who benefit from this. He practices what he preaches and pushes others to go deeper than they originally intended. In *The Sacred Us*, Justin demonstrates that God not only created us for this but has also given us a tool to help these relationships flourish and multiply. My hope is that this book is used by God to develop in you a passion for meaningful connection within your local church family that becomes so compelling that your spiritually disconnected friends are drawn into these relationships with you."

Sean Sears, lead pastor of Grace
Church, Avon, MA

THE SACRED

THE SACRED US

A CALL TO RADICAL CHRISTIAN COMMUNITY

JUSTIN KENDRICK

DAVID C COOK

transforming lives together

This book is dedicated to my sacred us: my brothers and sisters who have walked closely with me, seen all my flaws, and continued to patiently love me. To my friends who have sacrificed much and loved much. To all those who lived on Dayton Street, Pardee Place, and Earl Street, and all the other living rooms of community, who have engaged in the experiment of life together and are living it still—thank you.

For me, it started at Schwartz Hall, then moved to 111 Helen. Then came marriage, then the houses, the band, and the church. Now it has spread even further. We've learned a lot, and it definitely hasn't been perfect. But it's been worth it. And I am grateful. I'm looking forward to our next round of adventures, and there's no one I'd rather run with.

CONTENTS

**For more,
including group study material,
visit TheSacredUs.com.**

INTRODUCTION

This is a book about church ... sort of. It isn't about church history or church structures. It isn't really about church programs or church government either. Such books are helpful, and many have been written, but they aren't the topic of this one. This is a book less about the *things* of church and more about the *soul* of church.

At its core, this is a book about community. But we will explore more than friendships and small groups. It's a book that speaks to what I believe is one of the greatest needs of our time—to rediscover and rebuild the *sacred us*. The *sacred us* is a term I use to describe the transcendent community knit together by the Spirit of Jesus and more deeply bound to one another than natural family or best friends. It's that *thing* we all know is painfully missing in so many of our churches and in so many of our lives.

I don't claim to have all the answers about the sacred us. But I have tasted it, lived it, and realized that I can never go back to Sunday-morning smiles and cheap, impersonal hellos. For the last twenty years, I have done life with a small group of committed people—who became a large group of committed people. Through all the changes, the sacred us has endured and in many ways been strengthened.

This book begins by investigating the great problem of fake community that has defined our time, with instant access and online friends. It will then explore the source of deeper community and outline seven principles that can guide us as we consider a new course. The aim behind these principles is to bring tangible renewal to church community, reshaping it from the inside out from a semi-committed social group into a supernatural eternal family. The principles discussed are rooted in the practices of New Testament Christians, but their relevance transcends culture and time. At the end of each chapter, I'll share a few "Sacred Steps." These are practical action steps that we can use to help us grow.

> This is a book less about the *things* of church and more about the *soul* of church.

Most importantly, my prayer is that the principles outlined in this book push us into a different type of Christianity—where friendships are deeper, love is richer, and mission is realized. Some of the ideas in this book will make you uncomfortable and might challenge your basic assumptions about relationships. I know that many of them still make me uncomfortable.

They might dig up old wounds of failed community or force you to deal with past experiences when church leaders let you down. You might have to confront things that annoy you about others, and you won't be able to hide the ugly parts of yourself. But take heart. If you will begin building something deeper with a few people, God will use the sacred us to heal the broken pieces from your past. The process will be sloppy, imperfect, and full of challenges. But it is through this messy process that we will really learn to love. And love, of course, is the greatest and most sacred of God's gifts.

1

FRIENDLY BUT FRIENDLESS

"Friendship is the greatest of worldly goods.
Certainly to me it is the chief happiness of life."[1]

C. S. Lewis

"You can't be really human all by yourself, of course. You need
other people to talk to and listen to and share your secrets with
and laugh yourself silly with and, when you really get to know
each other well, even to be able to be silent together with
without embarrassment. That is what friends are all about."[2]

Frederick Buechner

"If you live to be one hundred, I hope to live to one
hundred minus one, so I never have to live without you."[3]

Winnie-the-Pooh to Piglet

"Turn to me and be gracious to me, for
I am lonely and afflicted."

Psalm 25:16

Do you have a group of close friends? Do these friends challenge your faith, strengthen your love for God, and stand by your side no matter what? Have your friendships been tested? Have you suffered together, rejoiced together, and seen God work miracles together? For too many Christians, the answer to these questions is a resounding *no*.

Living in the northeast corner of the United States during the first wave of the COVID-19 pandemic, in the spring of 2020, I had a tough time trying to stay positive. Everything was shut down. People were sick, some were dying, and fear was the currency of the day. The church that I pastor jumped into action and started serving the community with distribution of groceries and ministry to shut-ins.

But a second pandemic started to sweep through our nation as the months of isolation took their toll. Racial tensions peaked. Political tensions erupted. A few high-profile, nationally known Christian leaders were exposed for abuses of power and moral failures. It didn't take long before it seemed like everyone was upset about something. Fear led to frustration. Frustration led to anger and anger to offense. Soon the phone calls and emails started coming.

Someone in the church was offended that they hadn't yet received a call from a pastor. Another person emailed to tell us that we shouldn't wear masks because it was a government strategy to oppress people. Someone else reached out to tell us about how we weren't following COVID protocols closely enough.

I remember meeting with a group of our pastors and hearing horror stories about how so many good people were really struggling. Some were leaving the church. Some were just angry. We all felt it, and none of us were entirely sure what to do. It seemed like things that had been swept under the carpet for years were now taking center stage: insecurities, offenses, bitterness. The pandemic was accelerating and magnifying almost every problem, and our leaders were noticeably shaken. Since we'd launched the church nine years earlier, we had faced our share of challenges. But never like this.

Then came a moment I'll never forget. One of my best friends in the world, Matt DeCiccio, affectionately known as "Cheech," cornered me in my office after a long meeting about a disgruntled member of the church. Cheech and I have a lot of history together. We first met when we were teenagers. I was a passionate young leader, and he was a quad-riding, half-in, half-out church attender. He later made a radical commitment to Jesus, married one of my wife's best friends, and the two of us became inseparable. Cheech now serves as one of our pastors, and he was navigating some of the hurt and offense the pandemic had exposed. He closed the door behind him, took off his hat, and sat down.

"That was a tough meeting," he said.

"Yeah."

"People are so fragile. They're upset about everything."

"Yeah," I said again, tired and ready to fall down myself.

"Well." He looked up at me and smiled. *"At least we have each other."*

Those words meant more to me than I can ever say. Behind that short conversation was a lot of years, a lot of tears, a lot of laughs, and a lot of hope. *At least we have each other*—and that really did change everything.

We don't have a perfect friendship, and we don't agree on everything. But we have dreamed together, lost together, run hard together, and even burned out together. In a time when everything around us seemed to be shaking and crumbling, what my heart needed most was not a verse of Scripture or a big check in the mail. What I needed most was a companion. I needed a *friend*. And I am so glad that Cheech stopped by my office.

My kids grew up watching the *Toy Story* movies, and as a father with three sons, I was not surprised that the characters of Buzz Lightyear and Sheriff Woody became favorites in our home without much effort. In *Toy Story 3*, there's a scene toward the end of the movie when it appears that all hope is lost. Woody, Buzz, Rex, and the whole crew have been through a lot together, and they now find themselves trapped in a trash compactor, slowly headed toward a large furnace, where everything is being burned to ashes.

There's no way out. For a while, they scrape and claw, looking for an exit. But then the atmosphere changes, and across the faces of these toys appears a sense of resolve. Their lives are about to end, and there's nothing that they can do. The small group holds hands, and they look at death with courage because they're facing it together.

Cheesy, right? This is supposed to be a kids' movie. But if you were sitting with me that day in the movie theater, you would have noticed the tears uncontrollably running down my face. I was a grown man watching a cartoon with my elementary-age sons. Why was I crying?

It wasn't that I was worried about the fate of Woody and Buzz. I knew they would make it through the trial. This scene struck a nerve because it reminded me of one of life's deepest longings. It spoke directly to my story and reminded me that *I don't want to do this alone. I can't do this alone.*

The truth is that you weren't made just for *you*. You were made for *us*. But *us* comes with some significant challenges.

Not-So-Rugged Individuals

It seems that Americans in particular have an undying affinity for individualism. I can remember as a little kid hearing the stories of George Washington and Abraham Lincoln. Washington would return from battles with bullet holes in his coat but no wounds on his body. Lincoln would chop wood for hours every day and build log cabins with his bare hands. These two men, along with countless other men and women, loom over the American concept of success.

> The truth is that you weren't made just for *you*. You were made for *us*. But *us* comes with some significant challenges.

It's Theodore Roosevelt and the Rough Riders. It's Harriet Tubman and her amazing trips in the Underground Railroad. It's Amelia Earhart and her fearless flights. We use the term *rugged individualism* to describe these heroes. Didn't a group of iron-hard Pilgrims cross the Atlantic in the winter and start this nation in the name of freedom? They sure did. And they ate nails for breakfast.

Remember the Jason Bourne movies about the CIA agent who was determined to find out the truth of his past? Throughout the films, Bourne takes the most ridiculous beatings, jumping out of buildings, crashing cars, and getting shot—but he always bounces back. In one scene, he free-falls down a multistory stairwell and lands on the body of the guy he just killed. Then he gets up and keeps moving. Jason Bourne is a picture of the American prototype: *run hard, crash the car, rub some dirt on it—then get back up.* He doesn't need anyone. He's tough. And he is complete on his own.

Our obsession with individualism doesn't end with endurance or mental toughness. In order to feel like individuals who are in control, we also want *options*. We live in a world where our options are constantly expanding so that individual choice can be expressed. Choices help us feel powerful.

Do you want to watch a movie? Well, Netflix and its three-thousand options aren't enough. You need Hulu and Disney+ too. Do you want sugar in your coffee? Well, there's also stevia. Or honey? Or Sweet'N Low? Or monk fruit? We've come to believe that the more options we have, the more fulfilled we will be. So we keep creating more options with the hope of feeling more like we are in-control individuals, but is it working? Are people by and large *more* fulfilled?

In the midst of a culture that wants to feel in control, the church is often found scrambling for relevance. Many times, and without realizing it, Christians adjust the message of Christianity to appeal more directly to the individualism of our age. We tell people that the most important thing in life is a personal relationship with Jesus. And that's true. Isn't it?

But was your relationship with Jesus ever meant to remain *personal*, or is there a part of God that can be learned and experienced only in community? Can we even have a personal relationship with God if it's intentionally severed and isolated from interdependent relationships with others? If Christianity is simply about a *personal* relationship with Jesus, then why participate in church at all?

An emphasis on a personal relationship with God can unknowingly cause confusion around the purpose of Christian community. But church attendance doesn't ensure that true community is happening. Many followers of Jesus walk in and out of church each week and never deeply connect with anyone. Relationships are cordial but remain on the surface.

"Hey, Bob. How are you doing?"

"Doing great. You?"

"Never better."

"How about this weather, huh?"

Bob doesn't know you. He doesn't know the struggles you're having or the anxiety that's keeping you up at night. And you're not convinced that he would care if you told him, so you don't tell him. Nor do you know what's weighing on Bob. Too often we shuffle in and out of church like cattle on a farm or car parts on an assembly line, and this experience can leave us full of spiritual knowledge but void of real spiritual maturity. What's gone wrong with our Christianity?

Is it possible that when God created humanity, he never intended for us to be rugged individualists? What if we were actually designed to thrive only in the context of an intentional spiritual community? In our deep allegiance to individuality and our undying pursuit of autonomy we have lost something sacred. Our individuality has led to isolation. Our isolation has led to loneliness. And our loneliness has led to a profound emptiness.

Long before there were Facebook friends, studio apartments, and the culture of rugged individualism, God revealed to Adam the truth about human nature: *It is not good for man to be alone* (Genesis 2:18). If it wasn't good for Adam, are you sure it's good for you?

The New Leprosy

Pia Farrenkopf graduated from Cardinal Cushing Central High School just outside of Boston in 1983. She was one of nine siblings and an excellent student, being accepted into the National Honor Society and receiving a scholarship to the University of Massachusetts Boston. Pia never married, had a handful of friends, and stayed loosely connected to her many siblings.

On March 5, 2014, she was found dead in her car, parked in the garage of her home. Her body was discovered by two repairmen who were sent to the house with a foreclosure notice. Pia hadn't been stabbed or shot. The cause of her death was unclear. But one thing about this tragedy was even more unnerving: Pia Farrenkopf had not died the day that the repairmen found her. She had not died the day before. In fact, she hadn't died the week before, or even the year before.

> God revealed to Adam the truth about human nature: *It is not good for man to be alone.* If it wasn't good for Adam, are you sure it's good for you?

Medical examiners determined that Pia had died on or shortly after February 25, 2009, almost five years before her body was found. She was forty-four years old, with nine siblings, dozens of nieces and nephews, friends, coworkers, and neighbors. And no one noticed that she was gone for approximately 1,817 days.[4]

How does a middle-aged woman surrounded by acquaintances go *unmissed* and *unnoticed* for so long? The truth is that no one really knows. It doesn't seem possible, and yet *it is*. There are no clear answers in the story of Pia Farrenkopf, but her tragedy illustrates a much larger problem plaguing our culture. It's been called the leprosy of the twenty-first century. Our way of life has produced a world where people are friendly but friendless, where we are known by many but actually *known* by very few.

We go about our daily routines, buying coffee at the local shop and saying hello to a neighbor, but our lives are void of deep, substantive relationship. Then one day we disappear. But no one calls. No one really notices or cares enough to find out why. The grass gets long and the mail piles up. Soon, weeks have gone by, and no one takes the time to ask what happened.

It wasn't always this way in the world. Before the twentieth century, only 5 percent of households were made up of a single individual. Today, more than one in four Americans live by themselves. It's not that living alone is necessarily a bad thing. Sometimes it's the best thing. But as more and more people choose to live alone, something significant is shifting in our world.

In his groundbreaking book *Bowling Alone*, Harvard professor Robert D. Putnam chronicled the last fifty years of the collapse of the American community.

> During the first two-thirds of the [twentieth] century Americans took a more and more active role in the social and political life of their communities— in churches and union halls, in bowling alleys and

clubrooms, around committee tables and card tables and dinner tables. Year by year we gave more generously to charity, we pitched in more often on community projects, and … we behaved in an increasingly trustworthy way toward one another. Then, mysteriously and more or less simultaneously, we began to do all those things less often….

By virtually every conceivable measure, social capital has eroded steadily and sometimes dramatically over the past two generations.[5]

Studies have found that the majority of Americans today feel that no one in their lives really knows them well. Sixty-one percent of adults battle loneliness on a regular basis.[6] This isn't the experience of an isolated few. Rather, this is just normal life for most people. We often turn to social media or online connections hoping to find deeper relationships, but counterintuitively, researchers have found that the more social media you consume, the lonelier you feel.

Our digital connection is somehow perpetuating the problem. Social media platforms monetize our loneliness, as the desire for friendship grows, but the experience of having actual friends is never realized. Journalist Stephen Marche has studied this trend for decades and concluded:

We are living in an isolation that would have been unimaginable to our ancestors, and yet we have never been more accessible. Over the past three decades, technology has delivered to us a world in which we need not be out of contact for a fraction

of a moment…. Yet within this world of instant and
absolute communication, unbounded by limits of
time and space, we suffer from unprecedented alien-
ation. We have never been more detached from one
another, or lonelier.[7]

The future of our culture seems to be rapidly moving toward
even greater isolation. In a *New York Times* article titled "The Age of
Individualism," Ross Douthat wrote:

In the future, it seems, there will be only one
"ism"—Individualism—and its rule will never end.
As for religion, it shall decline; as for marriage, it
shall be postponed; as for ideologies, they shall be
rejected; as for patriotism, it shall be abandoned;
as for strangers, they shall be distrusted. Only pot,
selfies and Facebook will abide—and the greatest of
these will probably be Facebook.[8]

Douthat's statement is intended to carry a sense of comedy, but
the truth behind the statement stings. Look around. Take a moment
for personal reflection. How many close friends do you have? Do you
sense that deep inner tinge of loneliness? If your life is a scene from
Toy Story, is there a Woody or a Rex in your circle? Do you live in
healthy community with others?

Ernest Hemingway's stories, like *The Old Man and the Sea*, have
made him an American icon for generations. Hemingway was one
of the most successful writers of his time, earning a Nobel Prize
and a Pulitzer Prize, among other awards. He was known as a man's

man—fearless, independent, successful, and straightforward: the ultimate *rugged individualist.*

Yet Hemingway's internal life was far more complicated. He was a notorious womanizer, and by the time he had reached his sixties, he was unhappy in his fourth marriage. All of his wealth, fame, and success couldn't fill the void in his life. Surrounded by admirers and friends, it seemed Ernest Hemingway felt desperately alone. One night, he found himself methodically cleaning his favorite rifle, wrestling with his thoughts and the person he had become. Finally, he decided. He said "Good night, my kitten" to his wife in the other room, then later put the barrel of the gun in his mouth and took his own life. Rugged individualism had reached its inevitable conclusion. *It is not good for man to be alone.*

This combination of individualism, social isolation, and fake digital friendship has taught our hearts a lethal narrative: *People will leave you, so live like you don't need anyone. Make life about reaching your goals and maximizing your comfort.*

Soon, friendship itself slides down the priority list, below a successful career and personal happiness. We learn to value things over people. We learn to value comfort over connection. And above all, we learn to value ourselves over others. Every relationship is expendable, and as soon as it costs too much, we move on. Marriages are discarded. Friendships are forgotten. And our lives become a series of transactional interactions.

Do I overstate the problem? I am afraid that the problem might be far bigger than we realize.

These factors are producing what's been called "the age of the functional narcissist," where everyone is out for themselves and no one apologizes for it. In Greek mythology, Narcissus was the handsome young hunter who cared about himself above all else. One day, he saw his reflection in a stream and was mesmerized. He became obsessed with his beauty, but his obsession eventually led to despair. In the end, Narcissus took his own life. It's a tale that has become all too familiar. In the pursuit of fame, comfort, success, or status, we gain the world and lose our own soul.

The truth is that Jason Bourne isn't real. No one falls down a multistory stairwell and just pops back up. Facebook friends can't carry you through the most important moments of life. You need something more. Your spiritual growth is a team sport, and it was designed to work in the context of an intentional spiritual community. If you and I are ever going to overcome the cultural loneliness that defines our time, if we are ever going to avoid the fate of Pia Farrenkopf or Ernest Hemingway, we must learn a radically different way of living. We must be willing to give up some of our individuality and relinquish some of our options. We must sacrifice our comforts. On an even deeper level, we must allow God to reshape our view of *him*.

Does all of this sound extreme? It is. In fact, a revelation of the *sacred us* changes everything. But what do you really have to lose?

For many people, deep relationship is so uncomfortable because it means relinquishing control. You have to let people in. Maybe you've tried to have close relationships in the past, and you ended up with a broken heart. You trusted someone and they took advantage of you, and you don't want to risk the pain of being let down again.

Like Adam and Eve in the garden, being exposed can be terrifying. Or maybe you've been hurt by leaders in a church. This pain is real, and for some people it makes the idea of Christian community sound like a nightmare. Maybe you have never experienced healthy community. You've learned to lower your expectations and keep your distance because that's just all you've ever known.

What if I let people in and they just annoy me?

What if they think less of me when they see my imperfections?

What if community constantly interrupts what I want to do?

All of these hesitancies factor in to why we sometimes resist community, but I believe that the number one reason so many of us remain stuck in inch-deep friendships is that for some reason *it's just easier*. It's easier to put up a fence in the backyard than to regularly interact with your neighbor. It's easier to turn on the TV than to have a meaningful conversation with your spouse. It's easier to stare at your phone while you're in the elevator than to make eye contact with the stranger you're standing next to. We stay isolated because deep relationship requires that we stretch and change.

The Scriptures teach that "there is a friend who sticks closer than a brother" (Proverbs 18:24 NIV). When most Christians read those words, they immediately think of Jesus. We've been taught that the writer of Proverbs was telling us that God is the friend who sticks closer than a brother. But is God really the one the writer was referring to? I don't think so.

It's true that Jesus can be your closest friend, but I'm convinced that the author had something else in mind. He's telling us that the glimpse of friendship we see in Woody, Buzz, Rex, and the others is *real*. He's telling us that a band of brothers, a holy sisterhood, is not only possible—it's essential.

J. C. Ryle rightly noted, "Friendship halves our troubles and doubles our joys."[9] How many of us are living with a double portion of trouble and a half portion of joy simply because we're facing the darkest moments of our lives alone? But this is not what God intended. You can live in healthy community, and there is no joy like the joy of a close friend.

For me, few stories capture the essence of friendship like The Lord of the Rings, when the Ring of Power and the fate of Middle-Earth are entrusted to Frodo Baggins and his small group of companions. They fight orcs, trolls, and demons together, and they eventually overcome, destroying the ring and saving the world. In the final pages of the story, Frodo and Sam have reached what appears to be the end. Surrounded by the overflowing lava of a volcano, the mission has been accomplished, but it seems that it will cost them their lives:

> "Well, this is the end, Sam Gamgee," said a voice by his side. And there was Frodo, pale and worn, and yet himself again; and in his eyes there was peace now....
>
> And then Sam caught sight of the maimed and bleeding hand.
>
> "Your poor hand!" he said. "And I have nothing to bind it with, or comfort it...."
>
> "I am glad you are here with me. Here at the end of all things, Sam."[10]

It's that last line that sums up the entire Lord of the Rings trilogy most accurately. The story was never really about a ring, a hobbit, or a wizard. It was always about a fellowship. It was about being *here*.

Sam sees Frodo's bleeding hand and wants to help. But Frodo isn't worried about his hand, because he sees the care and love of his friend, and in the end, that is enough. In the same way, life was never supposed to be about your job, or your house, or your hobbies. Life is really about being *here*. It's about close relationship.

Take this final scene from Lord of the Rings and superimpose it over your typical experience at a Sunday church service. People are drinking coffee and chatting about the weather. It looks perfect. But under the surface, one couple is on the edge of divorce, while another person is in a life-and-death battle with depression. These people don't need just a cup of coffee and an encouraging Bible verse. They need deep friendship. But where can we go to find a community like that?

> Life is really about being *here*.
> It's about close relationship.

During the formative years of America, people began spreading out across the western half of the continent, and settlers formed new communities with very limited resources. It was in this context that the practice of barn raising became common, and it continues today in many Amish and Mennonite communities. All the able-bodied people from the area would come together to help a single family. No one was paid. No one was guaranteed help. But these settlers had formed a sacred *interdependence*, so barn raising usually included everyone.

Together, they would accomplish in a day what would otherwise take months. And raising a barn on a new property was far more than a construction project. It meant stability, safety, and opportunity for everyone. It strengthened the future of one family, which in turn strengthened the future of the entire community.

These settlers understood that their relationship to one another was more than transactional. They were a fellowship. In a sense, they were like a single body. Each individual part was connected to the other and ultimately dependent upon the whole. A barn raising was a time of great celebration because they understood that the barn they were building belonged to them all.

But of course, things have changed over the years. You don't see too many barn raisings on Wall Street or Main Street anymore. Many of us don't even know our neighbors' names. We're bowling alone, being swept along in the current of our social loneliness and isolation. But what would it take to change direction? What would it take to rediscover and reestablish real community?

In the most famous sermon ever preached, Jesus told his followers, "You are the light of the world. A city set on a hill cannot be hidden" (Matthew 5:14). He wanted us to know that God's plan for humanity is to establish a community of people who reflect and display his glory in the world. The English translation of the sermon can lead us to interpret it through the filter of our individuality, but Jesus didn't actually say *you* are a city on a hill. You aren't. He said *we* are.

In the original language, Jesus used the plural form of *you* to emphasize his point. He literally told them, "*Y'all* are the light of the world." Not just one of you—all of you, together. In fact, the entire Sermon on the Mount is not describing the individual pursuits of a Christian, but rather the collective ethos of a new community.

Paul picked up on this theme when he told the Corinthian Christians, "Now you are the body of Christ, and each one of you is a part of it" (1 Corinthians 12:27 NIV). The church was not created to be a gathering of autonomous individuals, and Christianity was never intended to work outside the context of a sacred community. Because community is not simply something God does—community is who *God is*.

— SACRED STEPS —

As you reflect on the content of this chapter, consider taking the following steps to grow:

1. Write down in a journal your ideal picture of friendship. What would it look like for you? What would it feel like? Turn your picture into a prayer, asking God to open up new and deeper relationships.

2. Create a list of reasons you distance yourself from others. Have you been hurt? Are you afraid of something? Invite God to speak to you and heal these hesitancies in your heart.

3. Think of one person in your life who you haven't been a good friend to. Initiate a conversation, and ask for their forgiveness.

2

THE THEOLOGY OF US

"The first relational statement made about the human race was that God did not design us to function as isolated units."[11]
Tony Evans

"I long, as does every human being, to be at home wherever I find myself."[12]
Maya Angelou

"A deep sense of love and belonging is an irreducible need of all women, men, and children. We are biologically, cognitively, physically, and spiritually wired to love, to be loved, and to belong. When those needs are not met, we don't function as we were meant to. We break."[13]
Brené Brown

"You're no longer strangers or outsiders. You *belong* here, with as much right to the name Christian as anyone. God is building a home. He's using us all—irrespective of how we got here—in what he is building."
Ephesians 2:19–20 MSG

Psychologists call it *belongingness*. It's the emotional need to be an accepted member of the group. Maybe you felt this need for belongingness when you were picked last for kickball on the playground in school. Maybe you felt its sting when your sixth-grade girlfriend broke up with you. Or maybe your sense of belonging came alive when you received the letter of acceptance from your first-choice college. Whether we realize it or not, so much of life is driven by an innate desire to belong.

It's one of the core desires at the center of the human psyche. This deep longing to belong is often the driving force behind our search for approval, intimacy, achievement, and power. We all want to fit in. We all want to be given special access and opportunity. We want someone important to tell others how important we really are.

And just as feeling like you're in the club can cause your spirits to soar, so feeling like you're on the outside can be devastating. I recently took a flight with a friend who is a Platinum member with American Airlines. I don't fly nearly as often as he does. Once we had gotten through security, he casually asked me if I wanted to hang out at the Admirals Club. I honestly wasn't familiar with what that was, so he led me to a side door where Platinum members of American Airlines could wait for their flights.

Normally when I fly, I take for granted the fact that I will most likely wait in long lines packed with strangers, use unkempt airport bathrooms, and pay a scandalous amount for a cup of coffee on the layover between flights. This is just normal, expected airline travel.

It might sound ridiculous to you, but when I walked into the Admirals Club, I felt like Harry Potter the first time he went through the magic door to Hogwarts. Behind this average-looking door at the airport was an amazing little world. There were comfortable chairs, an endless supply of free coffee, and clean, private bathrooms.

Then, as we went to check into our flight, my friend and I were informed that we had been upgraded to first class. As I sat in my oversized chair, I turned to my friend and said, "Being an Admiral isn't so bad."

A few weeks later, I took another flight, but this time I wasn't with that same friend. When I went to get a cup of coffee at the airport, the line wrapped around the coffee shop. When I went to use the bathroom, it was overrun with people. I couldn't even find a seat to sit in while I waited for my flight. Discouraged, I walked down the hall and looked up just in time to notice the little door leading to the Admirals Club. My access was gone. I was once again on the outside looking in. *I'm not an Admiral anymore*, I thought.

It turns out that many times in life, *belongingness* can be a little slippery. At one moment, you might feel like you've taken hold of it with both hands, and you really do belong, and then in an instant, circumstances change, and you feel like you're back on the outside looking in. It seems belongingness is less about *what is* and more about what *we feel is*.

Maybe you've experienced this reality when you introduced two of your friends to each other. Before you know it, they are hanging out without you. You don't mind them being friends, of course, but somehow their friendship now feels like a threat. Are you being replaced? Insecurity rises up inside you. Why is our sense of belonging so fragile?

Our hearts are constantly searching for belonging, finding it, then losing it again, then finding it again. Do you remember in high school when your tribe of friends were so close? You promised each other that you would be friends forever, but today that group has drifted, and you rarely talk. Maybe you had friends from college who were once so important to you, but over time you've fallen out of touch. Remember that guy from your first job? Where did he go?

This cycle seems to continue throughout life. Some people bounce from one romantic relationship to the next. Some people bounce from church to church or from job to job, and we often blame others for these changes. We blame our parents, our pastors, or the best friend who let us down. The more people I talk to, the more I see the pattern: in one way or another, *all of us* somehow feel like we are on the outside. What's wrong with us?

Is it possible to live every day with a deep sense of belonging? The Scriptures give a direct and emphatic answer: *it is possible.* The prophet Isaiah addressed the issue directly when he wrote, "But now, this is what the LORD says … 'Do not fear, for I have redeemed you; I have summoned you by name; you are mine'" (Isaiah 43:1 NIV). What does it mean to be summoned by God? It means first that we see him as he truly is.

Learning to Dance

What picture forms in your mind when you think of God? Is he an older gentleman with a long, flowing beard and a lightning bolt in his hand? Is he a mysterious force or a mighty cloud? How do you picture God in your mind? The mental image you hold of God will never reflect the revelation of God in Scripture until that image is intentionally reconstructed. This is because the picture of God in the Bible transcends anything our natural minds would create. What comes into our minds when we think about God must be reshaped according to what's been revealed by Jesus.

Long before Jesus walked the earth in flesh, the Jews understood God to be the Creator of all things. "In the beginning, God created …" (Genesis 1:1). He revealed himself to Moses as the great *I AM* (Exodus 3:13–15). God *is* and always has been. He is the unchanging, ever-present one. God revealed himself as the all-powerful, immutable, omniscient, omnipresent, sovereign ruler of all things. (See Jeremiah 32, Psalm 139, and 1 Chronicles 29, for example.)

But when Jesus began to teach, he emphasized a relationship with God that shocked and offended the religious leaders of his day. He taught, "Pray then like this: 'Our Father in heaven …'" (Matthew 6:9). Before God can be known as judge or master, he must be understood as *Father*. This relationship to us as Father puts all his other titles in proper context. He is judge. He is master. But first, he is Father.

Jesus reshapes our view of God with his emphasis on the *Father*, but he also made frequent claims to be one with the Father. He is the Eternal Son, equal to God. God is *Father*, but God is also Christ the *Son*, co-equal and co-eternal. This further stretches our understanding of God.

But God is not simply Father and Son. Jesus tells his disciples that he will send the Comforter, the Holy Spirit (John 14:16). God, therefore, eternally exists as the *Spirit* as well (2 Corinthians 3:17). Father, Son, and Spirit—one God, three persons. Three co-equal, co-eternal centers of awareness.

Biblical Christianity is not tritheism—the belief in three gods who work together. It is not modalism—the belief in one God who reveals himself in three different modes or forms. Rather, the Bible teaches the mystery referred to as *Trinitarianism*.

John Piper put it this way:

> There is one God, Father, Son, and Holy Spirit, three persons equal in divine essence and glory. The Father has, from all eternity, begotten the Son, meaning that the Father has known himself from all eternity with such fullness that the self which he knows is fully God—God the only begotten Son. And the Father and the Son have from all eternity (there are no beginnings in the eternal Godhead) loved each other, delighted in each other, with such a fullness that this infinite delight carries all the deity and stands forth as a third person—God the Holy Spirit.[14]

If your head is spinning, you might want to read it again. And read it a little slower the second time. The Trinity is the greatest mystery in the universe. God is not more fundamentally three than he is one, and he's not more fundamentally one than he is three.

Three persons, three unique centers of awareness—one essence. One God. And within the Trinity, Scripture gives us a glimpse into the different roles of each member. The Father *initiates*, the Son *complies*, and the Spirit *empowers*. We see this dynamic in the first story of creation. The Father speaks, the Son acts (as the Living Word), and the Spirit hovers over the surface of the deep, empowering the Word that was spoken.

Why am I going on about this? An understanding of the Trinity is not irrelevant theology just for seminary students and heady professors. The truth hidden in God's nature is the front door to understanding yourself and your deep need to belong. Because within the Trinity, God reveals something essential about life.

It's always the greatest desire of the Son to glorify the Father, and at the same time, it's the highest priority of the Father to glorify the Son (see John 17:1). Both Father and Son glorify the Spirit, who in turn glorifies the Son, who has been seeking to glorify the Father and the Spirit (see John 12:28; 16:14–15; Romans 11:36).

In other words, each member of the Godhead is eternally preferring, exalting, deferring, and honoring the others! God is one, and God is also three. He is within himself a living, vibrant, fulfilling community, in which each person of the triune God is eternally loving and serving the others.

Theologian Cornelius Plantinga Jr. described it like this: "The persons within God exalt each other, commune with each other, and defer to one another.... Each divine person harbors the others at the center of his being. In a constant movement of overture and acceptance, each person envelops and encircles the others.... God's interior life ... overflows with regard for others."[15]

The implications of this reality cannot be overstated. Sometimes we think of God and imagine a lonely individual sitting up in heaven looking for something to do.

From this perspective, God might have created the world because he wanted a project to occupy his time. But the God of the Bible has never been lonely for a moment. He is *within himself* a fulfilling relationship.

Imagine a scenario where you met someone who was so wonderful and amazing that you were willing to gladly give every moment of your life to honor, prefer, and serve them. Then imagine that as you began to do this, you discovered that this person thought you were so wonderful and amazing that they decided to give every moment of their life to honor, prefer, and serve you!

You might catch a glimpse of this kind of relationship through a connection with a best friend or your spouse, but even the greatest relationships on earth only brush the surface. This relationship sounds like heaven, and it sounds that way because it actually *is* heaven. The Father, Son, and Spirit have been in this type of relationship for all eternity. God *is* perfect community.

C. S. Lewis said it this way: "In Christianity God is not a static thing ... but a dynamic, pulsating activity, a life, almost a kind of drama. Almost, if you will not think me irreverent, a kind of dance."[16] Wait. God is a *dance*? What does that mean? It means that God is in constant motion, with each member of the Trinity forever seeking to love and serve the others.

In fact, God has illustrated the mysterious truth of his nature in all that he has made. Take, for example, the smallest building block on planet Earth: the atom. The atom has captured the imagination of scientists since its discovery, and within the atom there exist three fundamental entities: the proton, the neutron, and the electron. Interestingly, after decades of intense investigation, we have discovered that these entities seem to be in constant motion. Orbiting and moving around one another, the proton, neutron, and electron exist within some sort of dance! They are a community that is three and one at the same time and they echo the reality of the triune God.

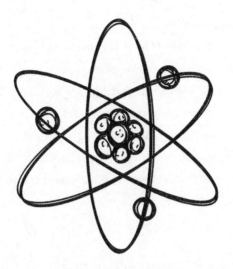

The fingerprints of God's triune nature are found not only in life's smallest building block—the cosmic dance is also found hidden in the stars. Astronomers tell us that right now planet Earth is not static. We are in motion, orbiting around the Sun. The Moon is orbiting around the Earth and the Sun at the same time. In fact, all the planets, moons, and stars in the universe are in motion, moving together in a perfectly choreographed dance through outer space. God is not a lonely, static individual. He is, by his very nature, a sacred friendship!

But how should this vision of God change the way we think about him? And how does the idea that *God is a dance* intersect with our deep desire to belong? An understanding of the Trinity is like a key that unlocks the door to life's greatest meaning. At the very core of all things, God exists not as an individual, but as a *fellowship of hearts*.

This means that relationship is not an afterthought in the universe. Relationship is central to all of life. In other words, the meaning of the universe *is loving relationship*. There is a God who is himself relational, and that God has befriended *you*.

Your deep, intrinsic desire to belong is not a peripheral ambition that can be satisfied with a membership to the Admirals Club. Your desire to belong flows from the core of who you are—the eternal part of you that ultimately, subconsciously, and insatiably longs for God himself. Augustine had it right when he wrote, "Our hearts are restless until they can find rest in You."[17] The need to *belong* must first be satisfied in God.

> Relationship is not an afterthought in the universe. Relationship is central to all of life. In other words, the meaning of the universe *is loving relationship*.

But the truth of the Trinity doesn't change your position as an outsider. God exists in a loving, dynamic relationship within himself, and on our own, you and I would still be on the outside looking in. That is, until we realize what Jesus actually accomplished for us on the cross. The incarnation—when the Eternal Son, the second person of the Trinity, became a human being—was always God's plan to invite us into his dance. When God the Son was made flesh, he permanently tethered himself to the human race. He is forever God, and now he is also forever man.

He lived a perfect life on earth, then died on the cross, exchanging places with you. His death paid your debt of sin before a holy God, and his resurrection proved that the debt was paid in full. Now, through faith in Jesus, God mysteriously sees Christ *in* you, and he sees you *in* Christ (Ephesians 1–2). This relationship is given to us by sheer grace (Ephesians 2:8)! We cannot earn it. We cannot work for it. The only way to access relationship with God is by trusting the work of Christ. We are brought into perfect relationship with God through faith in God's grace alone!

Your sin has been fully and forever forgiven through the shedding of his blood (Hebrews 10:14). And as the Father and the Spirit honor, glorify, and prefer the Son, so now in Christ the triune God will honor, prefer, and glorify *you*! Sound crazy? Taken out of a deeply biblical context, it is crazy. God certainly does not exist for us. Thinking like that will never lead to right relationship with God. We exist for him, to bring him glory. But we are not intrinsically beautiful or glorious. Rather, we are intrinsically sinful. So God makes us beautiful through the gospel in order that our bestowed beauty might reflect his grace. God glorifies us so that we might glorify him (see Romans 8:30 and 2 Thessalonians 2:14).

This is exactly what Jesus prayed to the Father in John 17. "I have *given them* the glory that you gave me, that they may be one as we are one—I in them and you in me—so that they may be brought to complete unity" (John 17:22–23 NIV). We are united with God through the grace given to us in Jesus. Jesus gave his glory to us, and God now treats you as his beloved child.

This is the essence of life's meaning and purpose. You were created *by* relationship. The triune God is your creator. You were redeemed *through* relationship. God accepts you on the merits of Jesus. And you exist *for* relationship. Your purpose for living is irrevocably connected to God and others.

These are important theological concepts. But how do these theological concepts translate into real life? It's one thing to know about community in our heads. How do we as Christians live community in our lives?

Dissecting the Disconnect

Understanding God as a dynamic community reframes the way we see him, but far too often it seems to end there.

Just because the Bible says that you are now cosmically connected to God through Jesus, it doesn't mean that this truth is real in your everyday experience. Most followers of Jesus don't live in a perfectly fulfilling, joy-overflowing relationship with God. In fact, for many of us, relationship with God often feels more like an idea than a reality.

Sometimes God feels distant. Sometimes our problems feel more real than his presence. Why is there an apparent disconnect between what Christ has provided and what we have received? The simplest answer is that most of us are dancing to a different beat. We've replaced God's rhythm with our own song.

Remember the picture of the atom, where each part is orbiting the other? Each part exists to prefer, honor, glorify, and defer to the other. The dance works because no single part puts itself first. The root problem in the life of most Christians is that we still see ourselves as the center of the dance. We think, act, and live as though life should revolve around us.

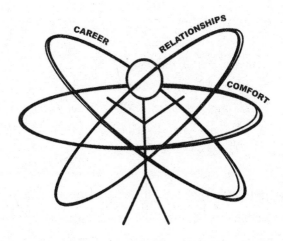

We love the idea of God radically glorifying, honoring, and preferring us, but we don't realize that the only way to step into the dance with God is to fully embrace the ethos of the dance. You can't stay at the center of your life and expect to experience real relationship with God. You must orbit your life around him, preferring, honoring, and deferring to him in all things.

This is exactly what Jesus was teaching us when he said that those who try to save their lives will lose them, but those who lose their lives for his sake will find them (Luke 9:24). He wasn't trying to punish us or rob us of joy. He was teaching us the path to real joy! The fullness of life and the reality of true belonging are found as we lose ourselves in God. To lose yourself in him *is* to perfectly belong.

Tim Keller made this observation:

> [God] must have created us to invite us into the
> dance, to say: If you glorify me, if you center your
> entire life on me, if you find me beautiful for who

I am in myself, then you will step into the dance, which is what you were made for.… You are made to center everything in your life on me, to think of everything in terms of your relationship to me. To serve me unconditionally. That's where you'll find your joy. That's what the dance is all about.[18]

To dance with God requires that you let go. Fully surrender. Lose yourself in him. Imagine what would happen if all the professing Christians in your community actually did this? What would happen if together we removed ourselves from the center of our lives and entered into a sacred dance with God? If we're honest, most of us don't like the idea of surrendering control of our lives. There's a part of our hearts that wonders: *How can I really be sure that God's way is best for me?*

A dance works only if one person leads and the other follows. If both partners try to lead the dance, the entire thing falls apart. And so God, anticipating our hesitancy, has already taken the lead. On the cross, God chose *us* over *himself.* He left his high position and took our low position. He gave it all, preferring and honoring us, and he did it long before we could ever reciprocate! He revealed his heart through sacrifice so that our hearts would have the evidence they need to trust him.

The Scriptures tell us exactly what would happen if we would enter the sacred dance on God's terms. In fact, it has been his dream from the dawn of time. "God has now revealed to us his mysterious will regarding Christ—which is to fulfill his own good plan. And this is the plan: At the right time he will bring everything together under the authority of Christ—everything in heaven and on earth" (Ephesians

1:9–10 NLT). God is building something special. He has been building it throughout history, and he is building it still, right now.

Remember that scene in the 2000 movie *Gladiator* when the Roman Emperor Marcus Aurelius takes his great general Maximus aside and shares with him his most intimate dream? It might be my favorite scene in the whole movie: an old man sharing his heart with the next generation. The emperor leans forward and says, "There once was a dream that was Rome. You could only whisper it. Anything more than a whisper and it would vanish."[19]

> The church is the sacred community.
> It's the very body of Jesus, his
> flesh and blood on the earth, and
> relationships between believers
> have supernatural potential.

Picture Jesus, the Son of God, sitting around the table with his twelve disciples. He gathers them close and then takes out the bread and the wine. I can imagine on that night he said something similar to his disciples as he explained God's eternal dream. *There once was a dream in the heart of God. It's called the church....* Then he revealed the secret of his sacred community. He took the bread and the wine. He said, "This is my body. *Eat*" (see Matthew 26:26). Through the cross, we have become one with him and one with each other. The *sacred us* was born.

The church was always meant to be far more than a social club. It was intended to be more than a place to disseminate religious information. The church is the sacred community. It's the very body of Jesus, his flesh and blood on the earth, and relationships between believers have supernatural potential. They can go deeper and wider than any other relationship in life.

It's through these relationships that we can know God, learn to fully know ourselves, and reveal the light of his glory in a dark world. As we take and eat of this gospel, Christ himself lives in us, we live in him, and we live in each other—made complete through connection.

— SACRED STEPS —

As you reflect on the content of this chapter, consider taking the following steps to grow:

1. Write down a time in your life when you felt insecure and like you didn't belong. Search the Scriptures for two or three verses that address that insecurity. Memorize the verse that resonates most deeply with you.

2. Make a list of things in your life that compete with your love for God. These might even be good things—like family or your career. After you have listed between five and ten things, turn each area over to God, making him first in your heart.

3. Discuss the content of this chapter with a friend. How does the triune nature of God change the way you think about him?

3

RE-CHURCHING
YOUR LIFE

"If you want to go quickly, go alone. If
you want to go far, go together."
African Proverb

"Christian community is more than just a supportive fellowship;
it is an alternate society. And it is through this alternate human
society that God shapes us into who and what we are."[20]
Tim Keller

"[God] created the church to meet your five deepest
needs: a purpose to live for, people to live with,
principles to live by, a profession to live out, and power
to live on. There is no other place on earth where you
can find all five of these benefits in one place."[21]
Rick Warren

"Just as our bodies have many parts and each part has a
special function, so it is with Christ's body. We are many
parts of one body, and we all belong to each other."
Romans 12:4-5 NLT

Two giants enter the stadium. Each man wears only a small loincloth. After a series of traditional rituals, the two lock arms. They both use every ounce of strength they possess in an ancient test of power, form, and speed. Although sumo wrestling has countless nuances, the ultimate goal is simple: *stay in the circle.*

In many ways, life is like a sumo match. There are pressures and enemies, and things are in constant motion. But what we sometimes don't realize is that around each of our lives there is a circle. And all around us the crowd cheers and calls. The pressure mounts and expectations build. Your responsibility is clear: *no matter what tries to push you out, stay in the circle.*

Sociologists call that circle *culture.* Drawn around every one of our lives there are customs, norms, habits, laws, beliefs, and information that form the circle of our culture. Why does red mean stop and green mean go? Culture. Why do we shake hands when meeting a new person? Culture. Why should you close your mouth when you chew? Why can't you wear jeans to the golf course?

Culture creates an invisible circle around your life. Like a fish swimming in a tank, every one of us is swimming in the culture of our time, and the pressure is always there to stay in the circle. There are things you can say and things you can't talk about. There are things you can do and things you shouldn't be caught dead doing. Of course, over time, culture changes; each generation it evolves and reshapes itself.

Every culture has redemptive elements that echo the heart and nature of God, along with toxic elements that pollute the environment of society. In our time, certain cultural ideals are gaining traction, while others are being washed away. For example, the insta-bility of our modern world has led to a greater desire for security. So we don't let our kids ride bikes to the local playground anymore. And if we do, they'd better wear a helmet. We install security cameras in our homes and theft protection on our credit cards.

Another example of our cultural ideals is our value of entertainment. We pay athletes millions of dollars to put a ball in a hoop, and we spend hours watching them do it. We value independence and privacy. We build networks and contacts. We expect our internet to always work, and it needs to work quickly. And we will usually pay more for good coffee. All of these are examples of cultural norms.

> Every culture has redemptive elements that echo the heart and nature of God, along with toxic elements that pollute the environment of society.

If you read this book a hundred years from now, you'll probably chuckle at how irrelevant these examples have become. Every culture has a circle that is constantly expanding and contracting, and every culture has a crowd shouting to each of us to stay in the circle. To step outside the circle will earn you the wrath of the crowd—just try to wear skinny jeans to a golf tournament. But it's not that everything about the circle is bad or must be rejected. Cultural norms are necessary for any society to function.

When God sent Jesus into the world and he whispered his eternal plan into the ears of his disciples, his intention was not to eliminate culture but rather to supersede it. He spoke of the kingdom of God, a way of life informed by heaven. His kingdom didn't come to imme-diately replace every aspect of the culture of the day. Instead, it came to reshape the human heart and grow like a seed until every decision, feeling, perspective, and desire had been radically reshaped by its values. The child of God understands the culture of the day, enjoys the benefits of that culture, redeems the broken pieces of the culture, but lives within the larger circle of the kingdom of God.

It was always God's intention that through his death and resurrec-tion, Jesus would inaugurate an entirely new way of life. Remember in the story of creation how God made Eve? He first created Adam, then put him to sleep and opened his side. Removing a piece of Adam, he formed Eve and presented the woman to the man (Genesis 2:21–24). Adam received his bride.

This story is a picture of the eternal plan of God in Christ. Just as God put the first man to sleep, so he put the second Adam, Jesus, to sleep. On the cross, Christ died and was then pierced in his side. God took from the side of Christ his very life, and from his substance formed a bride. And he calls his bride *the church*. It was never God's intention for his people to be confined or controlled by the cultural circle of their day. Instead, they were to become experts at moving in and out of the circle, always and above all, citizens of heaven. The church is something special, something eternal: a collective body of people—redeemed, forgiven, and reborn.

When Christians in the city of Corinth started arguing and dividing, the apostle Paul wrote to them and warned them: "You are still worldly. For since there is jealousy and quarreling among you, are you not worldly? Are you not acting like *mere humans?*" (1 Corinthians 3:3 NIV). These Christians were quickly taking offense. They were slow to forgive. They were divisive. In short, they were *human*. But Paul unapologetically expected more. Because of Jesus, you aren't *merely human* anymore. You are right now in the process of becoming more. You are becoming like God, whom we have seen in the last chapter *is himself* community.

Life Beyond the Circle

What's so different about followers of Jesus? What is this new community actually supposed to look like? We catch a glimpse of the uniqueness of the people of God in the second chapter of the book of Acts.

> All the believers devoted themselves to the apostles'
> teaching, and to fellowship, and to sharing in meals
> (including the Lord's Supper), and to prayer.
>   A deep sense of awe came over them all, and
> the apostles performed many miraculous signs
> and wonders. And all the believers met together in

one place and shared everything they had. They
sold their property and possessions and shared the
money with those in need. They worshiped together
at the Temple each day, met in homes for the Lord's
Supper, and shared their meals with great joy and
generosity—all the while praising God and enjoying the goodwill of all the people. And each day the
Lord added to their fellowship those who were being
saved. (Acts 2:42–47 NLT)

This passage of Scripture has served as a prototype for Christian
community for over two thousand years. Yet, though many Christians
have read it hundreds of times, we've somehow lost the essence of its
power.

It describes the early followers of Jesus as people who embodied
an *unusual devotion*. They were hungry for God—so hungry, in fact,
that they were willing to defy the cultural norms of the Jews and the
legal limits of the Romans just to gather and pray. They were often
rejected by their families or thrown into prison for their faith. These
early Christians chose commitment to Jesus over personal comfort
on an almost daily basis. Can you imagine a community today that
lived with this kind of unusual devotion, where people prioritized
the community itself over their own individual needs? It wouldn't
take long before a group like that caught the attention of a lonely
world.

The early church was also a community *marked by wonder* (Acts
2:43). Miracles were happening. People were being healed. The hard-
est hearts were changing and becoming open to God. These people

were more interested in worship gatherings than they were in politics, hobbies, or entertainment. God had captivated their attention.

They had all things in common and were selling their possessions and giving the money to those in need (Acts 2:44–45). They lived by a *dangerous unselfishness*. It was costly and inconvenient, but they gave anyway, compelled by love. And the truth of the gospel didn't stay in their church services. It found its way into their marriages and family life. It had what I call *living room application* (Acts 2:46). This group of new believers were practically working out the implications of Jesus' teachings in their daily lives.

Lastly, we are told they shared their meals with joy and generosity, constantly welcoming new people into the community (Acts 2:46–47). In other words, they were living *open lives*. They had widened their hearts in response to the love of God (see 2 Corinthians 6:11–13).

Now, this New Testament church was not a perfect, idyllic community. They still wrestled with sin, and they still made mistakes. But they were different. Consider the list of characteristics mentioned above: they lived with *unusual devotion, marked by wonder*; they practiced a *dangerous unselfishness*, with *living room application, opening their lives* to those around them. This community was stepping outside of the cultural circle, and their lives were changing the world!

Notice how these characteristics are in direct opposition to many of the values and virtues of our current society. We are taught by our culture to choose personal autonomy over radical devotion, entertainment over wonder, security over unselfishness, independence over vulnerability, and privacy over an open life. If an individual or a group of people tried to live by these kingdom virtues, they would have to deal with the surrounding society's constant pressure to conform. Yet previous generations of Christians did exactly that.

I love the description of the Thessalonian church: "We remember before our God and Father your work produced by faith, your labor prompted by love, and your endurance inspired by hope in our Lord Jesus Christ. For we know, brothers and sisters loved by God, that he has chosen you" (1 Thessalonians 1:3–4 NIV). This verse tells us that these early Christians lived with a faith that worked, a love that bled, and a hope that lasted. The inspiration that fueled their lives is right there in the text. They knew they were loved and chosen by God—and that one revelation changed everything.

Leonard Ravenhill once said, "One of these days some simple soul will pick up the book of God, read it, and believe it. Then the rest of us will be embarrassed."[22] In other words, how can we say that we believe in the truth of God's love and then remain so committed to the cultural circle of our age?

What if, together, you and I decided to step outside the circle? What if we chose right now to give our lives for a community bigger than ourselves? We know where the narrative of our culture leads—to loneliness, emptiness, and isolation. So why should we follow it any longer? Why not venture out into biblical community, with all its messiness and challenges? What do we really have to lose?

The Adventure of a Lifetime

When I met Jesus as a teenage kid in New Haven, Connecticut, I quickly found myself attracted to a relationship with God but tentative and reluctant about my relationship with the church. I read the book of Acts and fell in love with the idea of a sacred community, but the churches I interacted with just didn't connect with my heart in this way. So, I passionately pursued Jesus … but drifted little by little away from the church. Then something changed the day I met Shawn.

Shawn and I first connected at a Christian youth event, and he later invited me to come visit him at his ministry center. A few weeks passed, and a couple of friends and I made the drive from Connecticut to New Hampshire to visit Shawn. When we pulled up to the address, all my assumptions collapsed. There was no ministry center—there was just a big house with about twenty cars parked out front. But that perception was about to change.

We went inside and met Shawn's wife, along with some of the leaders of the ministry. They had a large home and a number of people living with them. And they were different. After a few hours of conversation, I was hooked. Their faith was vibrant. Their passion for God was palpable. They prayed for *fun*—sometimes long into the night. They loved God freely, not driven by guilt or obligation. Maybe most important of all, they did life *together*.

Shawn and his team ran the ministry school and an outreach center. But it was far more than that. They shared meals, went shopping as a group, and had fun together. It wasn't a cult—no one was forced or coerced into it, and they were committed to a historically orthodox theology of the Christian faith. Yet they embodied something that was fundamentally different from the casual Sunday Christianity I had become accustomed to. They looked and smelled a lot like the book of Acts, and I wanted more.

I remember coming home from that visit with my head spinning. What had I just seen? And what implications did it have for my life? I started my sophomore year of college with a new perspective. I was looking for opportunities to experiment with a deeper spiritual community.

Soon, the door opened, and I moved onto my college campus to share a room with three other new Christians. The four of us were as different culturally as you could imagine: one white guy, one black guy, one Puerto Rican guy, and one Indian guy. Yet all our cultural and racial differences never hindered our deep relationships. We studied the Bible together, prayed daily with each other, and had tons of fun together. We became more than friends. In the truest sense, we became brothers, and we grew exponentially in our spiritual lives.

By this time, I was committed to a life of biblical community, and there was no turning back. In my senior year of college, I shared a two-bedroom apartment with eight other guys, all young in our faith and pursuing Jesus together. It was a glorious mess. We ate meals together, prayed together, and carried each other through some of the craziest experiences of life.

I got married two weeks after graduating college, and my wife and I bought a two-family house in the city. Our commitment to living in community was only strengthened, and soon, we had two people living with us, along with Christian friends renting the other apartment in our house. Those were sweet times, learning to grow in our faith as we started our family.

A few months after we bought our first house, our best friends bought a house a block away from ours. We had a total of eight people living with us, and they had nine with them. We would gather for cookouts and worship services, practicing our faith in the context of friendship. But the experiment didn't stop there. We bought another house around the corner from the first, and some other people from our community got the house next to ours. Then another family got the house behind ours, and a fourth family bought the house on the other side.

From this growing group of people, we started our first church, and the community exploded from dozens of people to hundreds. Within the first couple of years of the church, more families moved into our area of the city, until we had twelve houses full of people living in close proximity—all of us in a four-block radius! Eventually, our family and a number of others moved out of those homes to launch churches across New England, but the vision for intentional community didn't stop. It has only gotten stronger as the church has continued to grow.

This all might sound a little crazy to you, but through this unorthodox, countercultural, mildly invasive passion for biblical community, God began *re-churching* my life. He started showing me that his plan to change the world has always been the church—a spiritual fellowship made up of people in process, created to glorify God and shine his light in the world.

In the Scriptures, the church is described as the bride of Christ. Remember, we came forth from him just as Eve did from Adam. It's also described as the family of God and the army of God. But maybe most frequently, the metaphor of the church used in the New Testament is that of a single, unified body.

Understanding the Body

Most Christians are at least mildly familiar with the analogy. Jesus is the head, and we are the body. This means that all Christians are connected to Christ and to each other. But before you assume that you've learned all the implications of this illustration, let's take a few moments for deeper consideration. What does it really mean to be the body of Christ?

I heard a story recently about a little girl who was scared of the dark. She came running into her parents' room one night, unable to sleep. Her mom sent her back to her bedroom, saying, "Don't be afraid, honey. You're not alone. God is always with you." The little girl shot back, "I know God is with me, Mom ... but I really need someone in my room with skin!"

This is what it means to be the body of Christ. The people of God are the skin and bones of Jesus, walking the earth today to make his presence known. What an honor and what a responsibility! But this truth goes even further. Paul wrote, "Just as our bodies have many parts and each part has a special function, so it is with Christ's body. We are many parts of one body, and *we all belong to each other*" (Romans 12:4–5 NLT).

We all belong to each other? Wait a minute. Something about that statement makes my individualistic mindset uncomfortable. I thought I *belong* to Jesus. Are we saying that my brother in Christ and my church family have a right or a sense of ownership over *me*?

The truth of the body of Christ teaches us that *it's impossible to stay connected to the head if you're disconnected from the body*. You can't have a personal relationship with Jesus if you're unwilling to have a committed relationship to his people. Christianity will never be an independent endeavor.

Consider, for example, the purpose of a hand. Its purpose is relevant only if the hand is connected to the body. All its value, power, and meaning are lost if it's severed from the body and lying on the ground. Yet most Christians don't see the value, power, and meaning of their lives connected to the church. We think about life as autonomous individuals, and we think of the church as an add-on to our already busy lives. But do you see now how unbiblical that way of thinking is? It's no wonder so many of us wander through life, unclear about our purpose.

> You can't have a personal relationship with Jesus if you're unwilling to have a committed relationship to his people.

Have you ever seen a body part disconnected from the body? If you have, you know it's never pretty. The beauty of the part requires connection to the whole. And so it is with your life. God has called you to something beautiful, but you will never find it apart from biblical community. And as we have seen, biblical community is not simply church attendance. It's more. It's the intentional practice of life together. Biblical community provides a new way of thinking about life and a new way of doing life. Throughout the book, I call this new way the *sacred us*.

In his letter to Christians in the city of Ephesus, the apostle Paul taught the church the difference between mature thinking and immature thinking. He warned that Christians can get stuck as spiritual infants, never growing in their faith (Ephesians 4:14). These immature believers are described as those who are tossed around by the waves and wind of life because of their immaturity. At one moment, they feel full of faith—but in the next moment, they're ready to give up. One day, they're committed to holiness. The next day, they're dabbling with sin. This is a picture of the spiritually immature.

But Paul made a distinction between the spiritually mature and the immature when he called the immature "infants" and the mature "a mature man" (Ephesians 4:13–14). He used the plural form to describe the immature, but the singular form to describe the mature. He was teaching that Christian maturity requires that you shift your thinking from *We are a bunch of separate individuals going to church* to *We are a single people, united as one.*

Immature Christians see themselves as separate individuals. They have an *individual mindset.* They have their own plans, goals, and dreams. But mature Christians see themselves through a *connected mindset.* They have learned to think about their life as a connected member of the body of Jesus. According to Paul, this way of thinking creates roots that keep you grounded. You're no longer tossed around by the wind and waves.

As you reflect on your own life, ask yourself, *Have I internalized the mindset of the spiritually mature? Do I view my life in the context of the community of Jesus, or have I lived my life in the circle of our culture—clinging to privacy, independence, and autonomy?* What holds you back from diving into deeper community? Is it fear? Unforgiveness? Past hurt? We all have our reasons. But in order to grow, we must move forward.

> Mature Christians see themselves
> through a *connected mindset.*
> They have learned to think
> about their life as a connected
> member of the body of Jesus.

The Scripture is clear: you *need* the people of God, and the people of God *need* you. The church grows as "each part does its own work" (Ephesians 4:16 NCV). This means that you are part of God's plan, and your unique contribution is essential to God's purpose.

Something to Give

God has designed his community in such a way that every believer in Jesus has an important contribution to make. This means that you have something meaningful to contribute. You may not be a worship leader or a pastor, but try not to think of "church" through a Sunday-morning, Americanized lens. It's not that our Sunday gatherings, our times of worship, or our sermons are bad. They aren't. They are a part of the universal church. But the community of God is *more*. Think of church as the *sacred us*. God has called you to be a part of his family, and he has given you at least four important contributions that only you can make.

Your Story. Maybe your journey to find Jesus was dramatic and it took decades. Or maybe you gave your life to Jesus at the age of five. Either way, you have a story. That unique story will connect, encourage, and challenge someone else. Only you have your story. Only you have faced your unique set of challenges. There is not a single story quite like yours, and it's a gift from God. He has called you to share it with others.

Your Strength. God has given you a unique strength. It's different from everyone else's. You may be weak in one area, but God has made you strong in another. You might be weak as a preacher, but you are strong as a pray-er. You might be weak as a counselor but strong as an encourager. God has given you a great strength, and he created the community of Jesus in such a way that the strength of one member can be passed to another. The strength you need is hidden in your brother or sister, and the strength you have is for someone else in God's community.

Your Service. God gives each of his children spiritual gifts and practical gifts to serve one another. He has also given you a unique sphere of service (2 Corinthians 10:13) that only you can fulfill. You might have a gift to organize, prophesy, serve, teach, or lead. Your service makes the people of God complete.

Your Sacrifice. Only you can make the sacrifice that God has called you to make. He has blessed you with a certain amount of money and a certain amount of time. If you don't make your sacrifice, you will miss out on God's fullness, the church will miss out on the gift, and the world will miss out on your witness.

The Principles of Authentic Community

What started in my life as four college friends in a dorm room became nine twentysomethings in an apartment. From there, two families opened up their lives, which soon became twelve houses in the middle of the city. This vision of intentional community continues to expand to hundreds of homes and rearranges the lives of all who embrace it.

In our journey of learning the *sacred us*, certain principles have emerged over time. A principle should be understood as an ingredient, a characteristic. It is a fundamental truth that guides the application of biblical community.

These principles work in various cultural contexts. They won't require that you live in a commune or move in with a group of monks. They won't require that you quit your job or change careers. But they will require that you rearrange your life. And they will pull you out of the circle. They will force you to confront your cultural narrative of autonomy and embrace the spiritually mature thinking of the body of Jesus.

They will also teach you to know God as you've never known him before. You will see his face in the face of your brother and feel his embrace in the comforting hand of another believer. And you will find yourself. Because God doesn't want to swallow up your individuality or wash it away. Unity does not mean uniformity. He has made you unique and special, but that uniqueness finds its full expression through deeper relationship with him and others.

The seven principles outlined in this book are not the musings of a philosopher. They aren't theories. They have been wrought by the invasive process of real life. The rest of this book will focus very little on structures or programs, as important as those topics are. Instead, we will explore the *substance* of community. What makes the *sacred us* unique? How do we develop a community like this that lives together as the body of Jesus?

I need to confess that I have not mastered these seven principles. Even as I write this book, I am keenly reminded of how far I have to go. I don't claim to have holistically or comprehensively listed all the principles of biblical community. I have learned seven, so I will share seven. There are people I have walked beside who embody many of these principles far better than I do, and that's really the point of community—to learn the heart of Jesus through one another.

If you will practice these principles and apply them in your context, they will inspire a different way of living. Your life will look less like your neighbor's and more like the book of Acts. Fellowship with God will deepen. Friendship with others will deepen. And God will use you to write the next great chapter in his story of *us*.

— SACRED STEPS —

As you reflect on the content of this chapter, consider taking the following steps to grow:

1. Read Acts 2:42–47 and make your own list of characteristics of the early church. Write down at least two things you can do differently in your life to follow the example they set.

2. Take time this week to reflect on your relationship with the local church. How can you do more than just participate in programs? How can you actually connect with the life of God in others?

3. Write down the specifics of your story, your strength, your service, and your sacrifice. Share it with a close friend and hold each other accountable to engage with God's people at a deeper level.

4

PROXIMITY PROVIDES OPPORTUNITY

"The physical presence of other Christians is a source of incomparable joy and strength to the believer."[23]

Dietrich Bonhoeffer

"You and I must make a pact. We must bring salvation back. Where there is love, I'll be there."[24]

The Jackson 5

"The God who is Divine community is known only in human community."[25]

David Benner

"Jesus said to them, 'Come and have breakfast.'"

John 21:12

Ten people in the middle of nowhere. Whoever lasts the longest wins $500,000. The contestants are allowed to choose ten survival items to bring with them. They can't bring food or guns. They will spend their days in the brutal wilderness of some obscure place. It might be Mongolia, Patagonia, or Vancouver Island. Each participant is given a satellite phone, and they can tap out at any time. But only the last person standing receives the prize.

There's one more important feature to this reality television series that has made it so difficult: each contestant is completely and utterly *alone*.

When the TV show *Alone* first came out on the History channel, it sounded to me like the most boring show ever imagined. Who wants to watch a bunch of random people film themselves alone? As it turns out, millions of viewers want to watch it, me included.

I first became intrigued with the series when a friend of mine showed me a video on YouTube of a guy who shot a moose with a bow and then lived off the meat for weeks. He ended up winning season 6. Soon, my sons and I were binge-watching season 1, placing bets on who would tap out last. The contestants chosen for the show are not the faint of heart. They are hardened survival experts from all over the world. Some have taught classes on wilderness survival for years. Others live with their families in the bush.

But *Alone* does something to these proven experts. Every season, many of them tap out after just two or three days. They aren't starving to death. They aren't getting eaten by wolves. Instead, they are caving and crumbling under the psychological strain of their isolation. Like Tom Hanks in the movie *Castaway*, who ends up building a close friendship with a volleyball, these wilderness experts often underestimate the impact of being completely alone.

The presence of another person fundamentally changes the mental state of the individual. We think differently and feel differently. Just one person introduced into your daily experience shifts your entire outlook on life. This is not news to any of us, and yet for some reason, most of us tend to withdraw from others, even when people are all around us. Think of the last time, for example, you flew on an airplane. It seems that as soon as people find their seats, everyone builds a technological fortress around themselves. The earbuds go in. The screens come out. We sit inches from the person next to us but often do our best never to make eye contact.

I recently sat across the aisle from a young twentysomething who was seated next to a man in his seventies. I watched as the cultural collision played out before my eyes. The younger man was quick on the draw. He had earbuds in and two screens out before the older man could sit down. But the older man was persistent. He didn't want a technological fortress. He hadn't adapted to the social withdrawal that's become so natural for most of us. So, he started talking to the young man. At first, the young man didn't respond, since his earbuds were in. Then slowly and reluctantly he pulled out one earbud and acknowledged the man.

This back-and-forth played out for the next two hours as the older man kept initiating conversation and the younger man kept retreating to his screens. Neither would surrender, so the battle raged until we landed.

Why is it that we've grown so comfortable in our protective social bubbles that we tend to disengage from the actual people in front of us? Why are we more concerned with some famous person's most recent social media post than we are with *being present* for the people right here?

A while ago, I was on vacation with my family in Florida, and we spent an afternoon by the pool. A new family had just arrived, and they had two boys my sons' ages, but the kids didn't leave their chairs for over an hour. Mom, Dad, and the two sons sat in chairs by the pool, all of them glued to their phones. They spent thousands of dollars to come to a beautiful place, and yet they were missing their vacation to scroll Instagram.

Most of our cars have five seats, but we usually transport only one passenger. People don't actually carpool. It's a nice idea, but no one wants to do it. Seventy-six percent of Americans drive to work alone every day. Think about this—we create a TV show that isolates people, participants leave the show because it's so hard to be alone, and then we get home and ignore the people who are supposed to be the most important to us. This doesn't make any sense.

> Somehow, all our connection has left us less connected, and all our accessibility has made us less accessible.

You've probably had the experience of sharing something significant and meaningful with a close friend or loved one, only to realize that they were responding to a text while you were talking. They didn't listen to anything you said. They looked up from their phone as you finished sharing your heart and responded with a blank "Huh?" Somehow, all our connection has left us less connected, and all our accessibility has made us less accessible. We've traded quality for quantity, and the return on investment is terrible. Something has to change.

The Ministry of Presence

What would you do for your closest friend? How far would you go to stay connected? Remember the old James Taylor song:

"You just call out my name and you know, wherever I am I'll come runnin', to see you again. Winter, spring, summer or fall, all you have to do is call and I'll be there, yes, I will. You've got a friend."[26]

Sometimes, it's not enough to pick up the phone or chat on FaceTime. Something powerful and irreplicable is exchanged when we share the same space. Being physically present with another person cannot be substituted with a digital device or a warm and thoughtful letter. Solomon told us this years ago when he wrote, "Better is a neighbor who is near than a brother who is far away" (Proverbs 27:10). There is more to being available than just picking up the call. You need to be *there*.

Years ago, I read a book by Frederick Buechner in which he told a story from his life. The story impacted me so profoundly I think it's worth sharing here.

> I remember an especially dark time of my life. One of my children was sick, and in my anxiety for her I was in my own way as sick as she was. Then one day the phone rang, and it was a man I didn't know very well then though he has become a great friend since, a minister from Charlotte, North Carolina, which is about 800 miles or so from where I live in Vermont. I assumed he was calling from home and

asked him how things were going down there only
to hear him say that no, he wasn't in Charlotte. He
was at an inn about twenty minutes away from my
house. He'd known I was having troubles, he said,
and he thought maybe it would be handy to have
an extra friend around for a day or two. The reason
he didn't tell me in advance that he was coming
must have been that he knew I would tell him for
Heaven's sake not to do anything so crazy, so for
Heaven's sake he did something crazier still which
was to come those 800 miles without telling me
he was coming so that for all he knew I might not
even have been there. But as luck had it, I was there,
and for a day or two he was there with me. He was
there for me. I don't think anything we found to
say to each other amounted to very much or had
anything particularly religious about it. I don't
remember even spending much time talking about
my troubles with him. We just took a couple of
walks, had a meal or two together and smoked our
pipes, drove around to see some of the countryside,
and that was about it.

I have never forgotten how he came all that
distance just for that, and I'm sure he has never
forgotten it either. I also believe that although as
far as I can remember we never so much as mentioned the name of Christ, Christ was as much in
the air we breathed those few days as the smoke of
our pipes was in the air, or the dappled light of the

woods we walked through. I believe that for a little time we both of us touched the hem of Christ's garment. I know that for a little time we both of us were healed.[27]

The first time I read Buechner's story, something reverberated deep within me. What kind of person drives eight hundred miles just to check in on someone? It sounds almost irresponsible. That way of living must be terribly inconvenient. Who would you ever do that for? Or maybe a better question is, *Have you ever done that?* Because a lot of us tell ourselves that we would do it, but we don't ever actually do it. We talk a big game, but when the moment comes, we often find a good reason not to get in the car and make the drive. The story underscores something that we all know but often forget: *presence matters.*

Just call, and I'll come running. It's true that you can't come running for everyone, but shouldn't we all be willing to come running for some? Shouldn't we be more than willing—shouldn't we actually do it?

Albert Mehrabian, a researcher of body language in the 1950s, made famous his finding that "the total impact of a message is about 7 percent verbal (words only) and 38 percent vocal (including tone of voice, inflection, and other sounds) and 55 percent nonverbal."[28] This means that communication is only about 7 percent what you say. It's 93 percent how you say it, how you stand when you say it, and how you look while you say it. In other words, connection between two people is dramatically compromised unless the two individuals are actually in the same room.

Being present means being available physically and emotionally. We're all thankful for Zoom, and it has its place, but virtual meetings are fundamentally inferior to physical interaction. For far too long, we've been only partially engaged, and our closest relationships can't move forward until we learn to fully engage.

The description of the early church in Acts 2 reveals how physical *proximity* was essential to the rapid growth of the church. We're told specifically that it was the habit of these early Christians to meet *every day* (Acts 2:46). Every day? Who has time for that? These believers gathered daily, either formally or informally. Sometimes at the Temple Courts, which was a social hub at that time, and other times in their homes, having dinner together.

It was so consistent that the proximity had a multiplicative effect. They opened up their schedules and their lives in a radical way, and the results were exponential. Proximity provided the space to learn, grow, and change. Growth was rapid and consistent because *proximity provides opportunity*. This is the first principle of biblical community.

Learning by Doing

For most people today, the idea of being consistently present and available to other Christians feels pretty unrealistic. Take a few moments and consider the potential disruption it would cause to your schedule. You have your career, and you're finishing up school. You've got young kids, and you still get together regularly with your friends from college. You have family commitments. Your son plays travel sports. You have a lot going on.

Life is busy for most of us, so the idea of creating regular space for Christian community feels like a dream. Yet, for all our busyness, the average American still finds the time to watch over four hours of television every day, along with spending countless hours glued to our phones. Maybe this is less an issue of busyness and more an issue of priority. The truth is that you have the space for biblical community in your life. The question is whether you will use it.

When my wife, Chrisy, and I moved to Earl Street in the Westville section of New Haven, Connecticut, we were in our late twenties and already had two kids. We had just started our first church, but we'd been experimenting with living in intentional community for nearly ten years. Our family bought a house with a small backyard, and some friends we knew bought the house next door. Soon, friends from our church owned the houses in front, back, and on both sides of ours. I know that to some people, this might sound like a nightmare—and it certainly came with its challenges. But in that season of life, at that stage in our church, this experience was integral in teaching us the importance of proximity.

We took down the fence. We invited people to take their kids on the swings in our backyard anytime. Before we knew it, *proximity* took on a whole new meaning. I would often get home from work and find thirty people in our backyard. Kids were running around. Someone was cooking on the grill. We would spontaneously start a game of Wiffle ball or football.

It wasn't long after we moved into that house that I felt *compelled* to buy a hot tub. What I mean by *compelled* is that I wanted a hot tub in the backyard ... but for strictly spiritual reasons. I wanted to be able to baptize people who met Christ in our neighborhood—at least that's what I told my wife when I first shared the idea. She graciously went along with it, and I found a hot tub for $400 on Craigslist. We transported it using my friend's pickup and dropped the hot tub on some wooden pallets in my backyard. Before long, our sketchy hot tub was fully operational and ready for use.

We did end up baptizing a number of people in that hot tub, but God also had other plans for it that I wasn't aware of at the time. Over the first year or so, the hot tub became a gathering place for me and a number of the young guys who lived nearby. Some of the guys were new to following Jesus. Some were single and preparing for marriage. Some were first-time dads, trying to figure out how to lead a godly family. We spent hours in that hot tub over the seven years we lived on Earl Street, often wrestling through many of life's toughest questions. We shared our hearts and laughed together. We held one another accountable to act on what we talked about.

The hot tub created a shared space that provided the opportunity to share life. It was a consistent meeting place. And we were present. The proximity provided the opportunity.

You will probably never live with Christian neighbors on every side of your home or drop a community hot tub in your backyard, but this principle must be applied to your life if you are ever going to experience the real power of community. People need to be physically close. Relationship needs to be regular. You need a consistent place to gather, and you need time to gather. You need to bump into each other often and create blocks of time that don't have an agenda attached to them. It's in these meandering moments that God steps into the relationship, and like Buechner found with his friend from Charlotte, it's in these moments that Jesus becomes real.

What would it take for you to rethink your schedule, creating consistent blocks of time with other believers? What is your next step? For you, the next step might be committing to a local church. Maybe you've been floating between various churches, unwilling to put down roots. Or maybe your next step is to host a small group regularly at your house. If these things are already a part of your life, then maybe you start a consistent meeting with an even smaller group for breakfast or coffee. Or maybe you invite someone to come and live with you in your spare bedroom. Proximity means that we are both physically and emotionally present. What could that look like in your context?

The Bible never gives us a direct command regarding how proximity should play out in our specific situations. Depending on your circumstances and stage of life, it will look different. It's looked different for Chrisy and me at various stages in life. But if you are ever going to experience the deep joy and power of biblical community, the journey begins with proximity.

Pushed to Grow

One of the great benefits that comes from doing life in close proximity to other believers is that the regular interaction makes it far more difficult to hide the ugly parts of your life. Anyone can put on a happy face for an hour on a Sunday morning. But if your marriage is a mess—or if your prayer life is nonexistent—proximity will flush you out of hiding. The principle also works in another, more internalized way. If you're struggling in your faith and you feel distant from God, nearness to other believers can carry you along until the issues are worked out in your heart and Jesus is made real to you.

The disciple Thomas is a great example of someone who battled with his faith but found Jesus again through community. After the resurrection, Jesus appeared to the other disciples, but Thomas was not with them. When they later told him about the experience, Thomas would not believe (John 20:24–25). Henri Nouwen observed:

> Although Thomas did not believe in the resurrection
> of the Lord, he kept faithful to the community of
> the apostles. In that community the Lord appeared
> to him and strengthened his faith. I find this a very
> profound and consoling thought. In times of doubt
> or unbelief, the community can "carry you along"
> so to speak; it can even offer on your behalf what
> you yourself overlook and can be the context in
> which you may recognize the Lord again.[29]

The name Thomas means "twin," and his struggle represents something that's true for all of us. In a sense, we each have a twin. We each are two people: one who struggles and another who believes. It's in community that the believing one is strengthened and connects with God.

In my senior year of college, when three friends and I got a two-bedroom apartment on Helen Street, it didn't take long before 111 Helen Street became a hub of activity. I led a guy to Jesus, and he needed somewhere to live. We had a little extra room, so he came to live with us. Then one of my other roommates had a friend who needed a place. He came too. Soon, we had nine guys in the apartment, all trying to learn what it meant to follow Jesus.

One of these guys, Brad, had come from a pretty rough background and just recently decided to follow Christ. Things kept disappearing from the apartment, and because so many guys were in and out, we had no way of knowing who was taking what. First it was food. Then somebody's watch went missing.

One day, only Brad and I were home, and I was about to get in the shower. Before I left my room, I felt a nudge from the Holy Spirit to count the money in my wallet. I hesitated. Why would God want me to check my wallet? I decided to do it anyway and saw that I had a twenty-dollar bill and a ten-dollar bill. I closed my wallet, set it on the nightstand, and got in the shower.

When I got out, I felt that nudge again to check my wallet a second time. Now there was only the ten-dollar bill. I got dressed and went to talk to Brad.

"Brad, did you take twenty bucks from my wallet?"

"No, man, why do you ask?"

"Well, because I'm pretty sure you did."

"Justin, I would never take money from you. We're Christians."

"Brad," I said, "the Holy Spirit has found you out." I proceeded to tell him how God had nudged me to check my wallet right before I went in the shower. His face went pale. He froze.

"I need you to give me back that twenty bucks," I said. With his hands trembling, he reached into his back pocket and took out the twenty. He gave it to me, telling me again and again how sorry he was.

Brad hadn't dishonored just me—he had dishonored God. And God used community to flush out his sin.

Unfortunately, Brad didn't make it much longer at 111 Helen Street. He decided to leave because he didn't want the junk in his life to be exposed. And this tendency to retreat exists in all of us. It's true that proximity will certainly highlight your flaws and expose your sin, but if you run toward the light rather than away from it, and if you show the same mercy to others that Jesus has shown to you, then proximity can be a powerful tool in God's hands. He will use the nearness of others to force you to deal with the secrets in your heart, and even though it will be painful at first, it will be joyful in the end.

But proximity doesn't just expose your issues; it also expands your love. In one of his most famous books, *The Four Loves*, C. S. Lewis outlined the four different types of love in the Christian life. Every one of these loves will play a critical role in your spiritual growth. The first three are pretty well known. *Eros* is romantic love. *Phileo* is the love between friends. Maybe most famous of all is *agape*—self-sacrificing, godly love.

> God will use the nearness of others to force you to deal with the secrets in your heart, and even though it will be painful at first, it will be joyful in the end.

But the fourth type of love is often overlooked. It's *storge* love—the love that grows slowly between family members. Storge love is essential to spiritual maturity, and it's often forgotten or even avoided in the lives of many believers.[30]

In the first three types of love, you choose the other person. You choose your spouse and your friend. But in storge love, the person to love is chosen for you. You didn't choose your grandma or your sister. And if you're honest, there are people in your family whom you would have never willingly chosen. They rub you the wrong way, and you don't naturally get along. But storge love is learning to love the one you wouldn't have chosen. It's learning to appreciate the one who rubs you the wrong way.

Tragically, it's storge love that is so often missing in the family of God. To avoid the uncomfortable process of growing in storge love is to miss out on some of life's most important relationships. More often than we realize, it is the person we wouldn't have chosen who becomes the most precious to us.

I learned this from Huey Lewis and the News. You may not know who that is, but they were a famous band in the 1980s. I got into listening to albums on vinyl for a while, and I found one of their records for a dollar at a thrift store. I bought the record because I liked one song. But you can't skip songs when you listen on vinyl—you have to listen to the whole record. Over time, the song I liked at first became my least-favorite song on the album. And it was the song I wanted to skip that turned out to be my favorite.

Many of us keep skipping people who don't look like the type of person we would choose to have a close relationship with, and we miss out on storge love. We look for people with the same hobbies, at the same stage of life, from the same background. If we don't find those people, we run. Storge love teaches us to stay rather than run, not because we like the person, but because we are next to them—until our heart widens and our love expands. Pretty soon we realize that we didn't know what we really needed. God knew, and proximity provided the opportunity.

But proximity does not just provide the opportunity to deal with sin or to learn to love others. Most importantly, proximity provides the opportunity to become more like God.

Maybe the most overlooked and under-considered characteristic of God is that he is adamantly committed to staying close. He is transcendent, above and beyond the created universe. Yet at the same time, God is immanent. This simply means that God is *there*. He is close. He is present. And his *thereness* was powerfully expressed in the coming of Jesus. *The Message* translation captures the essence of this idea: "The Word became flesh and blood, and *moved into the neighborhood*" (John 1:14 MSG). God moved in, and he isn't planning on moving out anytime soon.

The God Who Is There

In John chapter 21, we read the story of Jesus visiting his disciples after the resurrection. The story begins by telling us that after Jesus had met with Thomas and the others, he revealed himself by the Sea of Tiberias (John 21:1). Jesus was doing more than revealing himself as risen—they had already seen him alive from the dead. Jesus was revealing *himself*. He was showing his disciples who he really was, what he was really like, and how relationship with him really worked.

The story begins with the disciples spending the night fishing and catching nothing. This is a rerun of the first time they met Christ, when he filled their nets with a miraculous catch. In John 21, Jesus shouted instructions to them from the shore, and once again their nets were filled to overflowing. They hurried back to land to meet him, and by the time they arrived, he had already started a fire. Then he spoke the words that revealed his heart. "Come and have breakfast" (John 21:12).

Consider for a moment the implications of this little story. If you were going to make up a story about the Son of God risen from the dead, how would your story go? It would probably not involve Jesus casually strolling the beach and then cooking breakfast. It might involve some angels, a voice from heaven, and trumpets. It would most likely be dramatic and awe-inspiring. I know that's the story I would probably write. But Jesus revealed himself in maybe the most unexpected way imaginable. No fanfare, no parade. Instead, the Son of God made breakfast. What is he telling us about himself?

He wants us to see that he is not who we think he is. He's not distant, aloof, or uninvolved. He's not too busy for us. He is the God who wants to have breakfast. So, sit down. Relax. Let's chat about your plans for the day. Let's make time and space to just *be*. Because he is the God who is *there*.

Throughout the Bible, God is given several different names to reveal important aspects or elements of his nature. He is called the *Lord Who Provides* and the *God Who Is Our Healer*. But in the book of Ezekiel, the prophet ended his prophecy with a picture of the heavenly city. "And the name of the city from that time on shall be, The LORD Is *There*" (Ezekiel 48:35).

God names the eternal city *The Lord Is There*. It has always been God's plan, from all eternity past, to be *there*. It has always been his intention for us to know him as a God who is available, attentive, and present. "God is our refuge and strength, a very *present* help in trouble" (Psalm 46:1).

Because God is *there*, his *thereness* meets the deepest and most fundamental need in our hearts—the need to be loved by someone who will never leave. We are, in reality, never alone. And his nearness gives us the strength to be like him. We learn to be deeply available to others as we discover and internalize God's deep availability toward us. If God prioritizes the importance of being *there* for us above all his other options in the universe, then we must learn to imitate him and live our lives with *thereness* toward others. Proximity provides an opportunity to practice being there for others, and this practice makes you more like Jesus.

But it will come with a cost. I love how Jesus told his disciples to meet him in Galilee after the resurrection. Galilee is over seventy-five miles away from where they were staying in Jerusalem. There was no interstate to take or bus to ride. They had to walk the whole way. It reminds me of Frederick Buechner's friend who came to visit from Charlotte. Staying close requires that you go out of your way for the sake of relationship. Are you willing to do that? Are you willing to prioritize proximity with other followers of Jesus even when it requires going way out of your way?

> Because God is *there*, his
> *thereness* meets the deepest and
> most fundamental need in our
> hearts—the need to be loved by
> someone who will never leave.
> We are, in reality, never alone.

If you know the story of John 21, then you know that Jesus didn't come just to have breakfast. After they finished their meal, he struck up a conversation with Simon Peter. I'd call it a hot tub conversation. Remember that on the night before Jesus was crucified, Peter denied him three times, and the guilt and shame of his failure still hung over their relationship like a dark cloud.

Peter's confidence was shaken. He could hardly look Jesus in the eye. But proximity provides opportunity, right? Sitting around the fire that morning, Jesus asked Simon Peter three times, *"Simon, son of John, do you love me?"*

His three questions intentionally mirrored Peter's three denials. They were an invitation back into honest relationship. Through this conversation, Peter's heart was healed and his relationship with Jesus was restored. I wonder if he would have gone on to become the mighty apostle Peter we read about in the book of Acts if he hadn't had that conversation with Jesus on the beach. And how would that conversation have happened if Jesus hadn't come by for breakfast?

The truth is that some conversations never happen until you make the space and the time to just come close. Some of your favorite songs will never be found until you take the time to listen to the whole album. Some aspects of God are never made real until you experience them through the care, attentiveness, and sacrifice of another believer.

I learned the lesson of proximity the hard way through the loss and restoration of one of the most important relationships in my life. I met Rick when I was thirteen years old. He was the youth pastor at the church where I had met Jesus, and he went out of his way to help me grow in my walk with God. We used to meet every week at Dunkin' Donuts at 6:00 a.m. before school. We would take out the Bible, read it together, and talk about what the passage meant.

Rick gave me my first opportunity to preach and my first opportunity to lead. When I was seventeen, Rick asked me to be on the launch team and start a new church with him. It was one of the most exciting risks I had taken in my ministry life. God used our steps of faith, and a new church was born.

But years later, through a series of events, we found ourselves at odds. There were misunderstandings and offenses on both ends, and it seemed like there wasn't much hope of restoration. We tried, but we just didn't see things the same way. We were both asking God to open a door and restore the relationship, but nothing seemed to change.

More time passed, and my wife and I felt that it was time to sell our home on Earl Street. That was a big move for us, since Earl Street had been the place where so much intentional community had taken place. It was our training ground in the power of proximity. By this time, Rick had become a realtor, and I felt a nudge from the Holy Spirit to ask him to help us sell our house. Even though the relationship was on shaky ground, he immediately agreed, and we began the process of selling our home and buying a new one.

Our house sold quickly, and we finalized the contract for our new house. Everything was moving along smoothly until the closing on the new house was delayed a week. Then it was delayed another week. In all, the closing of our new house ended up being delayed for over nine months. But during those nine months of waiting, God was working. Because of the complications with our closing, Rick and I needed to meet dozens of times, and over the course of those multiple meetings, the walls between us slowly crumbled. We both asked for forgiveness. We both forgave. We were able to move forward, no longer at odds, but at peace.

What if the closing of my new house hadn't been delayed those nine months and all those extra meetings weren't necessary? Would the relationship have ever been restored? What if Jesus hadn't shown up that morning on the beach to say hello and make breakfast? Would Peter have ever been restored? What if we hadn't put a hot tub in our backyard and all those important conversations hadn't happened?

For far too long, we have been putting in our earbuds and ignoring the person in the seat next to us. We've been showing up five minutes late to church and escaping out the back a few minutes early to avoid uncomfortable conversations with others. But we can't live isolated lives and expect supernatural connection. If all your best friends live hundreds of miles away, you need to ask God for something more. We must intentionally invite others into our space on a regular cadence. We must make room for the people we don't naturally love. And if we will, God will work miracles.

What will you do to make more space? *Proximity provides opportunity.*

— SACRED STEPS —

As you reflect on the content of this chapter, consider taking the following steps to grow:

1. Track your social media consumption, TV consumption, and phone use for three days. Then put new limits on your life to support being more present. Do you need app limits on your phone? Do you need to have TV-free days?

2. Ask the three closest people in your life how you could be a better listener. Apply what you learn.

3. Examine your living situation. Do you live alone? With friends? With family? Find one or two new ways you can use the space where you live to create greater opportunities for spiritual relationship. Should you host a small group? Should you rent a room?

5

VULNERABILITY CREATES CONNECTION

"There is no way to have a real relationship without becoming vulnerable to hurt.... As you take in the truth of what [Christ] did for you—how loved and affirmed you are—you'll be able to let down your defenses in your own relationships with other people. You won't always need to guard your honor."[31]

Tim Keller

"I could never myself believe in God if it were not for the Cross. In the real world of pain, how could one worship a God who was immune to it?"[32]

John Stott

"We have spoken freely to you, Corinthians, and opened wide our hearts to you. We are not withholding our affection from you, but you are withholding yours from us. As a fair exchange—I speak as to my children—open wide your hearts also."

2 Corinthians 6:11–13 NIV

It was the fifth grade, and I was already becoming concerned about my image. Some of my buddies had girlfriends. Kids started caring for the first time if their hair was combed or if their feet smelled. I remember one time in late spring, it was going to be one of those New England days when it was too warm to wear pants to school but a little too chilly in the morning to wear shorts. So, I came up with an ingenious idea. I would wear my shorts *under* my pants. That way, if I got hot during the day, I could just slip off my pants and be ready to go.

At recess that afternoon, the sun was hot, and it was time to put my plan into practice. I took a quick break from kickball and stepped off to the side, then slipped down my pants. It was then that another kid saw me and yelled out, "Hey, everyone, Justin Kendrick is stripping on the playground!"

I tried to explain. I tried to quiet down the crowd. But things were in motion and there seemed to be no turning back. That afternoon I became known as the kid who took off his pants at school. I'd get stopped in the hallway by other kids I didn't even know. "Hey, Kendrick," they would say, "I heard you pulled down your pants ..."

This is not the reputation you want to have in the fifth grade. I remember making a vow to myself after that experience: no matter how practical it might seem, I was never going to wear my shorts under my pants again—and I never did.

Ego management. The never-ending, full-time responsibility assumed by the vast majority of people is to protect, enhance, and support self-image. We spend countless hours every week on ego management, oftentimes not even aware that we're doing it.

I will catch myself in ego management from time to time. I wore the dark shirt because it makes me look thinner for that lunch meeting. I mentioned in the conversation an important person I know, because mentioning them makes *me* feel important. I exaggerated how much I worked last week so I could appear busier than I actually am. I obsessively keep mints in my pocket because I'm terrified of being in a conversation and having bad breath. What's wrong with me?

A while ago, my wife and I put our house on the market, and we had a friend come over and take some pictures for the realtor. Of course, we cleaned the house meticulously before she came. But even with a clean house, I found myself intervening.

"Don't stand there. I think if you stand here, it will make the backyard look bigger … Can we get one from this angle? It hides the garage door that needs to be replaced …"

When my friend was done taking the pictures, she did some magical editing and adjustments to opacity and color. In the end, the photos *sort of* resembled the house we were selling. Once they were posted, I started feeling a little guilty. Had I pushed things too far? Will people feel tricked when they show up and walk through our home?

My guilt was assuaged as soon as Chrisy and I started walking through other homes that were for sale. We'd walk in and quickly realize that the pictures we'd seen had made these houses look far better than they actually were. Everyone was massively deceiving the buyer! Everyone was editing the photos and making their house look like a palace!

Of course they were. Because we're all in the business of ego management. It's why you take thirty photos but post on social media only the one where the light catches you just right. And when you decide which one to post, the deciding factor is not how good your friend looks—it's how *you* look. It's why you buy another pair of shoes even though you have twenty pairs in your closet.

There is something inside us all that is constantly chasing an image. We're constructing airbrushed versions of ourselves to gain the approval of the world around us. Pull back a layer, and beneath this editing and posturing lies a deep insecurity. I've found it in myself more times than I can count. It may take a different form each time, but ego management frequently finds a way to sneak back in.

Fully Exposed

To be vulnerable means to be susceptible to hurt, to be open or exposed. How comfortable are you with vulnerability? How willing are you to admit it when you're wrong? How do you respond when those around you recognize your inadequacies or mistakes?

It seems most of us have a deep aversion to exposure. We feel like we have something to hide—that if we were fully ourselves in front of others, they would never accept what they saw. Psychologists call this *impostor syndrome*, and studies have found that an estimated 70 percent of people wrestle with these feelings at some point.

We posture, exaggerate, and camouflage. We make ourselves out to be more than we are. Some people feel like they aren't pretty enough. Others feel like they aren't successful enough. Some people walk around like roosters, always strutting and flaunting. Others walk around more like mice, scampering into the shadows anytime they are exposed. Where does this natural impulse toward insecurity come from?

It comes from a deeply rooted sense of *shame*. George Bernard Shaw once famously observed, "We live in an atmosphere of shame.

We are ashamed of everything that is real about us; ashamed of ourselves, of our relatives, of our incomes, of our accents, of our opinion, of our experience, just as we are ashamed of our naked skins."[33] Psychologist Carl Jung called shame "the soul-eating emotion."[34] Like a tapeworm in your stomach, shame has a way of eating away at you from the inside out.

Remember Ernest Hemingway and his novel *The Old Man and the Sea*? In the story, the fisherman, Santiago, feels the need to constantly prove his worth. No matter how many great fish he has caught, something inside of him says that he's only as important as his last catch. "The thousand times that he had proved it meant nothing. Now he was proving it again. Each time was a new time and he never thought about the past when he was doing it."[35] Every day, Santiago has to get out of bed and prove his worth.

Journalist Judith Shulevitz called this phenomenon the "inner murmur of self-reproach."[36] Have you ever heard that inner murmur? The voice on the inside that tells you that you aren't quite *enough*? I know I have. But where does it come from? And what can be done about it?

The Scriptures leave little mystery about the origins of shame. The answer is found in the first story. As soon as our ancestors chose a life of independence from God over holy dependence on God, they immediately became painfully aware of their own *nakedness*. "Then the eyes of both were opened, and they knew that they were naked" (Genesis 3:7).

The word translated "knew" in this text means more than just a cognitive knowledge. It's the same word used to describe the intimacy between Adam and Eve that produced children. When the author wrote that they *knew* they were naked, it meant that nakedness had

become a part of them—a part of their psyche. And their first incli-
nation was to cover up and hide. They hid behind fig leaves, then
behind trees in the garden, then behind excuses. But none of their
hiding places could cover their shame.

Something inside of you is telling you that you aren't enough.
There is an inner murmur of self-reproach that has been whisper-
ing in your ear all your life. Your defense mechanism is to create an
elaborate fig-leaf covering to protect yourself from this inner accuser.
You might build your identity around accomplishments, titles, an
attractive appearance, or a thousand other status symbols. But the
result of your fig-leaf mentality will be a life with a thousand "contacts" in your phone or "friends" on your social media platform, but
no real relationships. You will never feel connected.

In 2 Corinthians chapter 6, Paul encouraged the Christians in
Corinth to move out from behind their shame and insecurity and
step into a life of intentional vulnerability. He warned them not to
live *restricted* lives (2 Corinthians 6:12). This word *restricted* means
that their hearts had been tied up. The internal connections or path-
ways between them and God, and them and others, were narrow.
Paul instructed these believers to *widen their hearts*.

But widening our hearts doesn't sound very appealing to many
of us. We've spent our whole lives trying to build a wall of protection
against feelings of shame and inadequacy. If we were to widen our
hearts, we'd be risking exposure.

We have accepted a subconscious conviction that goes something like this: *If anyone saw you for who you really are—if they saw
your weakest moments and your deepest secrets—no one could ever love
you. No one could ever respect you after all that you've done. Your only
option is to keep up appearances.*

> The same restrictions that
> shield your heart from being
> deeply hurt also stop your heart
> from being deeply loved.

Maybe you've tried vulnerability in the past, but rather than being loved and accepted, you were judged. Like me, before long, maybe every kid in fifth grade was talking about how you pulled down your pants. Your reputation was tarnished. People made up rumors about you. And you took a vow never to put yourself in a vulnerable position again.

But there's a dark side to living behind a fig leaf. The same restrictions that shield your heart from being deeply hurt also stop your heart from being deeply loved. You can't be both emotionally safe *and* fully alive at the same time. So, your fig leaf ends up creating a prison, where you always feel alone. No one really knows you. You don't really know anyone, and your life becomes a shadow of what God intended for you.

C. S. Lewis wrote:

> To love at all is to be vulnerable. Love anything, and your heart will certainly be wrung and possibly be broken. If you want to make sure of keeping it intact, you must give your heart to no one, not even an animal. Wrap it carefully round with hobbies and little luxuries; avoid all entanglements; lock it up safe in the casket or coffin of your selfishness.

But in that casket—safe, dark, motionless, airless—
it will change. It will not be broken; it will become
unbreakable, impenetrable, irredeemable.[37]

You can't stay in your safe, protective cocoon. You must learn to widen your heart (2 Corinthians 6:13). The English Standard Version of this verse uses the word *widen* as opposed to *open*. Opening your heart doesn't sound so bad, since opening takes a lot less construction. I can open a door with the turn of a knob and then close it anytime I want. But to *widen* a doorway is now a construction project. It requires cutting, sawing, and breaking. Widening hurts. But this is how we learn the second principle of biblical community. *Vulnerability creates connection.*

Without great vulnerability, there can be no great connection—not between you and God and not between you and your brother. Relationships will always remain an inch deep until someone is willing to be vulnerable. You must risk exposure and reveal your weakness. You must confess your sin to your brother.

There's an inherent paradox in vulnerability. We tend to celebrate it in others but fear it in ourselves. We seem to be inherently attracted to honesty and transparency in the life of another person, seeing it as a sign of great strength in them. But when it's our moment to be vulnerable, we tend to consider vulnerability as a sign of weakness. Have you ever decided to share something deeply personal with another person, and as you were sharing it you found yourself editing the story? You're taking out the parts that feel most dangerous. You're adjusting the picture just enough to save face. You aren't free. You're still living with a narrow heart.

There's an inherent paradox in vulnerability. We tend to celebrate it in others but fear it in ourselves.

But Paul modeled for us a different way. He wrote, "We have spoken freely to you ... and opened wide our hearts" (2 Corinthians 6:11 NIV). What an amazing way to live! He wasn't hiding behind any fig leaves or enslaved by the opinions of others. Somehow, he had silenced the inner murmur of self-reproach. But how is that possible?

The Tale of Two Kings

The Old Testament story of Saul and David is a powerful example of the tension between insecurity and vulnerability. Both men were chosen from obscurity in Israel and launched onto the national scene. Saul was appointed king. David became his greatest general. But the insecurities in Saul led to his undoing, and he eventually disqualified himself from leadership. One day while Saul and David were returning from battle, the women sang songs about both men. In their songs, they attributed more success to David than to Saul. Saul couldn't handle the comparison, and soon he was making plans to have David killed. He started throwing spears.

Saul had a narrow heart. He couldn't bear someone else being more successful than him. Eventually, his insecurities eroded any sense of integrity in his life. He died by falling on his own sword—which, figuratively, is always the end for those who live by comparison.

Contrast his life with David's life. The writers of the Old Testament did not sugarcoat David's imperfections. He made some massive mistakes. Yet even in his ugliest moments, David exhibited a vulnerability and transparency that is breathtaking. Maybe that's why God called him "a man after his own heart" (1 Samuel 13:14). David was both strong and weak. He was confident and vulnerable. He would write in one of the psalms, "My enemies will turn back in the day when I call. This I know, *that God is for me*" (Psalm 56:9).

What a stunning sense of confidence, especially in the midst of his own failures. How did David live with such a wide heart? Gene Edwards made the following observation about David: "He seemed to grasp a deep understanding of the unfolding drama in which he had been caught. He seemed to understand something that few of even the wisest men of his day understood.... God wanted a broken vessel."[38]

God doesn't want you to hide in your shame. He doesn't want you to invest in a beautiful Armani fig-leaf covering. He wants you to be vulnerable, but in order to do that, you must abandon your false self, which finds its sense of worth through comparison or personal accomplishment. You must learn not to crumble when you look stupid or when you're misunderstood. But where can anyone find confidence and courage like that?

David and Saul are not the only two kings we need to compare. Prophetically, they serve as an arrow pointing to the more important comparison: the comparison between King *Jesus* and King *Self*. These two kings jockey for position in every one of our hearts. King Self wants to sew fig leaves and throw spears. King Jesus wants to deal with your nakedness. King Self wants to build a long list of accomplishments. King Jesus wants to convince you of his love. King Self wants to feed off comparisons. King Jesus wants to teach you who you really are.

It's only King Jesus who can silence the inner murmur of self-reproach and once and for all set you free from shame. He can teach you to be vulnerable and build deep relationships with others. But there is only one way with King Jesus. The apostle Paul outlined the way:

> Everything else is worthless when compared with the infinite value of knowing Christ Jesus my Lord. For his sake I have discarded everything else, counting it all as garbage, so that I could gain Christ and become one with him. I *no longer count on my own righteousness* through obeying the law; rather, I become righteous through faith in Christ. (Philippians 3:8–9 NLT)

If there is anyone in the New Testament who *should* struggle with a sense of shame, we'd expect it to be Paul. Before becoming a Christian, he hated the church and worked tirelessly to see Christians arrested and killed. Imagine the inner dialogue that must have occurred after Paul met Jesus. Imagine the guilt and the memories that would replay in his mind. Maybe this is why he called himself the greatest sinner (1 Timothy 1:15; 1 Corinthians 15:9).

Yet by the time he wrote his second letter to the Christians in Corinth, Paul was living with a wide-open heart. He wasn't hiding from his past. He wasn't walking around with a dark cloud over his head. He was free. No shame. No guilt.

What happened? Paul had experienced the Great Exchange. He gave Jesus his record—both the good and the bad—and freely received the record of Christ as a gift. "God made him who had no sin to be sin for us, so that in him we might become the righteousness of God" (2 Corinthians 5:21 NIV). Jesus took Paul's sin, and Paul took Jesus' righteousness. Paul no longer put *any* confidence in his own worthiness. Rather, his heart found perfect peace through the gift of grace.

Is this your experience with Jesus? Have you found that deep sense of assurance and confidence?

Philip Yancey wrote, "Grace does not depend on what we have done for God but rather what God has done for us. Ask people what they must do to get to heaven and most reply, 'Be good.' Jesus' stories contradict that answer. All we must do is cry, 'Help!'"[39]

What could happen if we all stopped crying out, "Look at me!" and instead started crying out, "Help!"? What could happen if we allowed God's grace to be what it actually is—free? Tony Evans defined grace as "all that God has done *for* you, independent *of* you."[40]

You can't add to God's grace. In fact, if you try to, you will end up destroying the gift. God protects your heart from ever striving or trying to earn his love by requiring that you receive his grace for free. God's gift of grace removes your credentials from the equation and bestows on you what some scholars have called an "alien righteousness." It's alien because it comes from outside of you. By faith, God now views you through the righteousness of Jesus. And all of this was accomplished because God did the unimaginable.

He became human—became *vulnerable*. Let this thought simmer for a moment. He was beaten. He was stripped naked. He was hung on a cross, fully exposed. People looked at his naked, bloodied frame and mocked him. God became vulnerable. He took your nakedness so that you could take his robe of righteousness. He loved you—even as you were sewing on the fig leaves.

It's at the cross where we find the truth that rewrites the internal story of our hearts. You are loved by God, even with all your warts and shame. Tim Keller added:

> To be loved but not known is comforting but superficial. To be known and not loved is our greatest fear. But to be fully known and truly loved is … what we need more than anything. It liberates us from pretense, humbles us out of our self-righteousness, and fortifies us for any difficulty life can throw at us.[41]

This is where we find the strength to be vulnerable. Everyone knows that blazing a trail through the woods is hard. Walking a path that another person cut is far easier. Paul was able to be radically vulnerable with others because he'd found the path of Christ. Jesus went first. He modeled vulnerability—and when his love fills your heart, you can be radically vulnerable too. Even if some people reject you or mock you, you can still have a deep sense of confidence and acceptance. And with vulnerability you can build the deepest, most satisfying relationships in the world. This is why Christian relationships have the potential to go deeper than any other human relationship—because they walk the path of King Jesus. *And vulnerability creates connection.*

Practice Makes Permanent

How can we learn to open up and be vulnerable? There's really only one way: *you have to practice.* Every time you step out and honestly share something about yourself that could be potentially damaging to your image, you recalibrate the scales of your heart. You add a little more weight to your identity in Christ, and you take a little power away from your insecurity.

A few hundred years ago, God used John Wesley as one of the key leaders in what has become known as the Great Awakening. During a relatively short time, hundreds of thousands of people turned to Christ in Europe and North America.

Many people know about John Wesley's powerful preaching, but he is less known for what the old Methodists used to call the "band meeting." This was Wesley's small-group model—it was his secret sauce. He encouraged all Christians to be involved in a band meeting. These groups usually consisted of three to five people of the same gender who would meet at least weekly. They would go through a list of questions every meeting. One question asked, "What known sins have you committed since our last meeting? What temptations have you met with?" Clearly, these groups didn't beat around the bush. This line of questioning leaves little room to hide. Either you embrace vulnerability or you don't. When was the last time you attended a group like that?

This type of brutal transparency has played a critical role in my spiritual life since I first met Jesus. It started with a few friends from high school, then it found new expression with my three roommates in college. Together, we would confess sin and be honest about our struggles. Later, I formed a group like this with the elders in my church.

About two years into pastoring, I met Bill. Bill is thirty years older than me and was the senior pastor of a church for most of his life. He visited our church one day and found me after the service. We knew each other peripherally at the time. "Justin, I think we should get together," he said. "I'm a spiritual director, and I meet with pastors on a monthly basis. Is that something you might be interested in?"

I didn't know what a spiritual director was, but I was more than willing to meet. Since that day nine years ago, Bill and I have met every month. In our meetings, I invite him into the deepest, darkest corners of my thoughts. Sometimes it feels so awkward, but the promise of the Scripture has proven true: "Confess your sins to each other and pray for each other so that you may be healed" (James 5:16 NIV). Forgiveness for sin comes from Jesus. But *healing* comes as we confess our sins to one another.

But not all vulnerability is created equal. Sometimes people will be vulnerable with others simply to gain sympathy or attention. They want the spotlight, and talking about their problems is one way to accomplish that. Too often, immature Christians use vulnerability as another tool to feed their own need for attention, but this is the exact opposite of God's purpose.

There is, of course, the possibility of oversharing. I recently bumped into an acquaintance who I hadn't seen in years. I gave him a big hug and said, "It's so good to see you. How are you doing?" I stood there stunned while for the next ten minutes he shared with me about an enema he had received and then a procedure on his anus that had left him with a tender bottom. I didn't know what to say. We went from "good to see you" to the intimate details of his buttocks in less than a second.

Oversharing can silence a conversation and hinder deep relationship. You don't have to share every detail with every person. But you do need to share the important details with a few, and you must learn to guard against editing out the specifics that make you feel embarrassed. Because through vulnerability, God intends to build a new type of community.

Deeply Connected

After Paul challenged the Corinthians to widen their hearts, he went on to write, "Make room in your hearts for us. We have wronged no one, we have corrupted no one, we have taken advantage of no one. I do not say this to condemn you, for I said before that you are in our hearts, to die together and to live together" (2 Corinthians 7:2–3).

Paul was expressing the purity of his motives, and he was giving us a picture of a beautiful community. He told the Corinthians that they were *in his heart*. He wasn't speaking allegorically. Because Christ dwelled in him and Christ dwelled in them, and together they were one body with Christ, the Corinthian Christians were actually *in* Paul's heart. They were cosmically, spiritually, supernaturally one. And because of Christ, so are we.

Paul used a phrase that sounds like it was stolen straight out of a Three Musketeers movie: *to die together and to live together*. All for one—and one for all. Who talks like that anymore? Doesn't he know that chivalry is dead? We live in the world of contracts and deals. We live in the world of dog-eat-dog, beat-you-to-the-top. But what if it didn't have to be this way? What if we are called to something more?

Does that sound too good to be true? Remember, Paul's love toward the Corinthians wasn't being reciprocated; that was why he wrote the letter. But their failure didn't stop him from being vulnerable. Because Paul knew that vulnerability creates connection, and through his vulnerability, he was sure he could win their hearts.

> When you are willing to let others in, God makes your heart bigger. And *every time you widen your heart, God deepens your joy.*

Paul ended this section of the letter like this: "I am acting with great boldness toward you; I have great pride in you; I am filled with comfort. In all our affliction, *I am overflowing with joy*" (2 Corinthians 7:4). What was he so happy about? As far as we can tell from his letter, the Corinthian church was a mess. But his joy wasn't dependent upon their performance. Paul had learned the power of vulnerability, that when you are willing to let others in, God makes your heart bigger. And *every time you widen your heart, God deepens your joy.* Through vulnerability, Paul felt more connected to God and more connected to others. He was fully alive.

But that connection and joy is not possible until you take a risk. You must embrace the danger of being known, with all your flaws and imperfections. You must stretch, take a chance, and confess your struggles, risking exposure and even embarrassment. But if you risk vulnerability, you will begin to sense a deeper connection with God and others, and a new community will start to form. Hearts will interlock. Compassion will grow. Love will become real. Something sacred will be born out of your brokenness.

Vulnerability creates connection.

— SACRED STEPS —

As you reflect on the content of this chapter, consider taking the following steps to grow:

1. Share something with a close, trusted friend that you have never shared before. Invite them into a part of your story that they didn't know.

2. Isolate one area of sin that you struggle with. Ask a mature Christian of the same gender if you could be accountable to them to grow. Commit to reach out to them anytime you face that weakness or temptation.

3. Begin to meet regularly with a committed group of two or three other Christians. Like John Wesley and his group, share your spiritual successes, failures, and questions.

6

DISCIPLESHIP SETS DIRECTION

"Effort and courage are not enough
without purpose and direction."[42]

John F. Kennedy

"Research has shown that a lot of what people desire
in life, such as healthy lifestyles, is actually 'contagious.'
… If they are surrounded by people who are healthy,
that is contagious as well. They are supported and
not thwarted … [they] catch the 'sickness.'"[43]

Henry Cloud

"You are the average of the five people
you spend the most time with."[44]

Jim Rohn

"I've got my eye on the goal, where God is
beckoning us onward—to Jesus. I'm off and
running, and I'm not turning back."

Philippians 3:14 MSG

He walked on the moon. There aren't too many people who can put *that* on their list of life achievements. Buzz Aldrin had been gone from planet Earth for eight days, three hours, eighteen minutes, and thirty-five seconds. But the world he came back to was fundamentally different from the one he left.

When the Apollo 11 mission successfully returned to Earth on July 24, 1969, President Nixon called it the greatest week since creation. This small team of three men had accomplished the impossible, and for the rest of their lives, they would be treated like more than mere mortals.

But with his new status, Buzz Aldrin also discovered a profound sense of emptiness. His whole life had been built around high achievement, but what's left to achieve for a man who has walked on the moon? Once the immediate euphoria of his success died down, Aldrin began spiraling. "I was suffering from what the poets have described as the melancholy of all things done."[45] Soon, his marriage started to buckle. He turned to alcohol. He battled depression and eventually suffered a mental breakdown. The moon was not enough, or maybe it was too much. His life no longer had direction, and without direction, life stops working.

Remember the movie *Groundhog Day*, where Bill Murray plays Phil Connors, a television weatherman who gets trapped in a time loop, reliving February 2 again and again? This is a vivid picture of a life trapped in the routines of a purposeless existence. It's the same cup of coffee, the same commute, the same work, the same evening routine. Day after day, nothing seems to change. There's no higher goal. There's no bigger plan.

Some of us live every day lacking a sense of direction, while others try to create a sense of direction in life through some future goal or accomplishment. Maybe you're reading this right now and you're getting married later this year. Maybe you're next in line for a big promotion. You might be looking forward to that vacation or the big project you're about to complete. These are all good things, but what will happen once you've obtained them? If you reach your goal, get the promotion, finish your education, marry that special someone—if you set foot on the moon—will that be enough?

Where is your life *really* going? Is there a bigger direction behind your life? Many of us go to great lengths to avoid these questions. Russian author Leo Tolstoy found great success at a young age. He completed the original version of *War and Peace* in 1863 at the age of thirty-five. What does the author who wrote *War and Peace* do next? How do you top that?

Later in life, Tolstoy wrestled deeply with a lack of direction. He described his great struggle as an abyss.

> *I could not attach a rational meaning to a single act of my entire life....*
>
> What will come of what I do today and tomorrow? What will come of my entire life? ...
>
> Is there any meaning in my life that will not be destroyed by my inevitably approaching death? ...
>
> My deeds whatever they may be, will be forgotten sooner or later, and I myself will be no more. Why, then, do anything? ...
>
> I cannot even tell whether I can see anything down below in the bottomless depths of the abyss over which I am hanging and into which I am drawn.[46]

Buzz Aldrin, Phil Connors, and Leo Tolstoy have more in common than you might imagine. They all found themselves circling the mountain of life, unable to satisfy the deeper ache on the inside. High achievement isn't enough. Comfort and status aren't enough either. Your life needs a better answer.

In the 2014 film *Fury*, Brad Pitt plays First Sergeant Don "Wardaddy" Collier, a leathery battle-hardened tank commander in Germany during World War II. He and his team of four men take on countless battles and eventually end up on an assignment to protect a strategic crossroads from enemy advancement. On their way to the crossroads, they are ambushed, and the larger group suffers massive casualties, leaving only their tank to fulfill the mission.

> High achievement isn't enough.
> Comfort and status aren't enough
> either. Your life needs a better answer.

When they reach the crossroads, their tank is immobilized by a land mine. An entire battalion of German soldiers is approaching, and the team must decide if they will run for their lives or take on the Germans against impossible odds. All five men decide to stay. Four of them lose their lives, with only Norman, the youngest and newest member of the team, living to tell the tale.

The first time I saw the movie, I watched it with a small group of my closest friends. We left the theater that night, and something hung in the air as we walked through the parking lot and got back in the car to leave. *Fury* had touched a nerve, and we all knew it. There was something in us that wanted to be in that tank.

We all want to be on an assignment bigger than ourselves, fully engaged in a worthy cause. And we want to be assigned to a cross-roads—something we've been called to fight for and protect. And maybe most of all, we want to fight alongside others for something that really matters. We need a *collective cause*.

C. S. Lewis said it best when he wrote, "If I find in myself desires which nothing in this world can satisfy, the only logical explanation is that I was made for another world."[47] We were created with a desire that the highest ambitions in this life just can't satisfy, because God made us in such a way that our hearts instinctively turn in an eternal direction. We want immortality. We want life beyond this world, and we want to experience that life with a committed group of like-hearted people.

The apostle Paul articulated this deeper desire when he wrote, "I count everything as loss because of the surpassing worth of knowing Christ Jesus my Lord" (Philippians 3:8). Paul realized that the highest ambitions in life can't meet our deepest need, and he described the overarching direction of his life a few verses later. "I press on toward the goal for the prize of the *upward call* of God in Christ Jesus" (Philippians 3:14). Paul gave us a better answer to life's deepest question of direction. You have an *upward call*. But he didn't want to go there alone. That's why he said a couple of verses later, "Brothers, join in imitating me" (Philippians 3:17).

Simply stated, the upward call of every Christian is to be conformed to the image of Jesus. "For those God foreknew he also predestined to be *conformed to the image of his Son*, that he might be the firstborn among many brothers and sisters" (Romans 8:29 NIV). For centuries, Christians have called this *discipleship*. Discipleship is living every moment of your life as a student of Christ. But it's more than a personal pursuit. Jesus always intended to bring many brothers and sisters with him. And this collective cause sets a new direction for life.

The truth is that we will never experience spiritual growth or understand how it works until we realize that discipleship and community must walk together. New Testament professor Robert Mulholland wrote:

> There is a temptation to think that our spiritual growth takes place in the privacy of our personal relationship with God and then, once it is sufficiently developed, we can export it into our relationships with others and "be Christian" with them. But holistic spirituality, the process of being formed in the image of Christ, takes place in the midst of our relationships with others, not apart from them.[48]

If *you* are ever going to reach the upward call of God, then *we* must do it together.

Thinking Differently

Once Paul talked about the *upward call* that we have in Christ, he then wrote, "Let those of us who are mature *think* this way" (Philippians 3:15). He was trying to establish for us a new way of thinking about everything.

Imagine your mind as an ecosystem. An ecosystem is a group of interconnected elements that form the environment of a given area. This includes things like geography, vegetation, weather patterns, and animal life. All these elements work together to form the ecosystem. Sub-Saharan Africa, for example, has a particular ecosystem. The wilderness of Alaska does too. If one element of the ecosystem is removed or tampered with, it can have major implications for the whole.

Maybe you remember in the early 1990s when scientists began the Biosphere 2 experiment. They created a mini-Earth—a giant bubble with the capability of recycling its own air, water, and waste. This three-acre glass dome was supposed to be a world independent of the world. It contained 3,800 different plant and animal species, and in 1991, eight scientists committed to move into this mini-Earth.

But the experiment was a massive failure. It ended up revealing how fragile a healthy ecosystem really is. First, the honeybees and hummingbirds died. Then, the ants and cockroaches began to multiply. Oxygen levels started to plummet, and mice were showing up everywhere. Biosphere 2 went down in history as one of the most expensive failures of modern science.

In between your ears there is an ecosystem. It's made up of your thoughts, beliefs, and values. It informs what you see when you look in the mirror. It tells you what things are worth pursuing and what things are worth ignoring. Without Jesus, the ecosystem between your ears is painfully imbalanced. Sin distorts everything, adding too much value to things that don't deserve it and taking value from things that do. Sin makes the human psyche unstable, full of insecurity, doubt, shame, and fear. The cockroaches are running rampant, and the hummingbirds are extinct.

Your thoughts about life can't find their proper balance until the *upward call* of the gospel reorders the ecosystem of your mind. *Everything* is a loss compared to knowing Christ. To know him is everything. Do you see how radical this way of thinking is? Do you see how different this is from the world around us?

Discipleship requires that we intentionally find people who are living lives devoted to Jesus and follow their example. Paul clearly modeled for us this different way of living when he said, "But I do not account my life of any value nor as precious to myself, if only I may finish my course and *the ministry* that I received from the Lord Jesus" (Acts 20:24). Too often, we think of *ministry* as something reserved for pastors and leaders in the church. But we define it too narrowly. Ministry is simply a life devoted to Jesus and committed to serving others. This means that regardless of your occupation, *you* are called to ministry.

> When *becoming more like Jesus* is the greatest purpose and primary direction of your life, you can find a unity with other believers that's impossible otherwise.

In fact, God has assigned a ministry to you that only you can fulfill. You have an area of influence assigned specifically to you (2 Corinthians 10:13). It includes the people you know, the abilities you have, and the opportunities that come your way. According to

Paul, fulfilling your ministry is more important than staying alive. It's your highest aim, your upward call.

And this upward call can't be lived out alone. Since we are the body of Christ, we can fulfill our calling only when we do it in concert with the people of God. It's here that we learn the third principle of biblical community: *discipleship sets direction.*

This third principle makes Christian relationships fundamentally different from all other relationships in life. The principles of proximity and vulnerability will work in any relationship, but discipleship makes Christian relationships different. It establishes a collective cause that ties us together beyond our hobbies, personalities, and interests. When *becoming more like Jesus* is the greatest purpose and primary direction of your life, you can find a unity with other believers that's impossible otherwise. Discipleship sets direction.

The Compound Effect

After coming to faith in Jesus as a teenager, I found my first Christian friends in the youth ministry of my new church. At first, we didn't seem to have very much in common. We came from different backgrounds and had different interests. Then one day, a girl named Lindsey invited a group of us over to her house for a prayer meeting. I brought my guitar. At the time, I didn't know very many Christian songs. The first time we met, there were about ten of us gathered at the house. I played the couple of worship songs that I knew, and each of us began to pray. Then something amazing happened.

The presence of the Holy Spirit became tangible. One kid started crying. Someone else got down on their knees. What I thought would last fifteen minutes stretched past two hours as a small group of teenage kids sought God with all their hearts. We met the next week. And the week after that. Those prayer meetings continued for over a year, and it was my first taste of biblical community.

I learned that community creates a compound effect in the process of spiritual growth. If you can stay around spiritually hungry people, it's only a matter of time before their passion gets on you. As each person lives as a disciple of Jesus, the growth of one inspires the growth of another. Soon, spiritual growth becomes irresistibly contagious.

Did you ever notice in the New Testament that we are told to sing to *one another* (Ephesians 5:19)? At first glance, this feels strange. But singing worship songs is not just for you and Jesus. Your song to God does something inside of *me*, and my song to God does something inside of *you*. Hearing you sing to Jesus will make me love him more. When a group of people wholeheartedly aim their lives at Jesus and then gather with that purpose in mind, the speed of spiritual growth compounds.

But God doesn't just give us the power to encourage each other's hearts—he also gives us the power to release each other's callings. Maybe you've read the story of David and Jonathan. These two friends shared a sacred bond. Most people are familiar with David, the famous Bible character who killed Goliath and went on to become Israel's most successful king. But few realize that we never would have heard of David if there hadn't been a Jonathan. David's best friend paved the way for his success, and when David was at his lowest point, it was Jonathan who got him out of the funk.

> And Jonathan, Saul's son, rose and went to David
> at Horesh, and *strengthened his hand* in God. And
> he said to him, "Do not fear, for the hand of Saul

my father shall not find you. *You shall be king* over Israel, and I shall be next to you." (1 Samuel 23:16–17)

Notice the boldness in Jonathan's declaration. He told David without hesitation that he would be the next king. Jonathan spoke right to David's fears, and the result was that David was strengthened in God! Do you see that? *Jonathan's words took the strength of God and transferred it into the heart of David!* God has put such a profound power in friendship that one believer can release the power of God in the life of another believer through their words.

This is so important, because there are going to be times in your life when you don't have the strength to continue. Who will track you down and find you in your place of hiding to strengthen your hand? And whose hand are you strengthening through the power of your words?

As I reflect on my walk with God so far, it's nearly impossible for me to quantify the impact my closest friends have had on my life. If it weren't for them, I'm not sure if I would still be a pastor. I'm not sure if my marriage would be healthy. Nearly every area of my life has been shaped by the powerful influence of my closest relationships.

Life is often hard, and the Bible never promises us a life without trial. But God uses the trials to reshape our character, and he brings others into our lives to walk with us. When, like David, your trials lead you to an empty cave, you need a Jonathan who will track you down and speak life over you. This is how your calling becomes a reality.

Do you have a group of close friends who stand with you through the trials? Do they regularly inspire you to love God more? Do they set your calling in motion by speaking words of hope and life? You can't get far without a group like this.

But real friendship must go in both directions. Do you play this role in the life of someone else? If you took time to reflect on the last year of your life, can you identify moments when you stood with a friend and held them up? Is this the type of friendship you offer to others?

For some of us, relationships like this might sound like a fairy tale. But it doesn't have to be. You can experience this. You can initiate this. And if you want to see it grow in your life, it will require that you embrace an uncomfortable love.

Uncomfortable Love

If we are going to build deep and authentic relationships, and if we are going to actually become more like Jesus, then we must learn to love each other enough to frequently engage in confrontation. This is what the writer of Hebrews meant when he wrote, "Let us consider how we may spur one another on toward love and good deeds" (Hebrews 10:24 NIV). Notice that the writer uses the word *spur*. That's the pointy thing on the boot of a cowboy that he jams into the horse's side when the horse won't move. No one really enjoys a spur in their side. So how is godly confrontation supposed to work?

When I lived in the two-bedroom apartment with nine Christian friends, we learned right away that not everyone in the house held the same standards of community. Four of the guys in the apartment were paying the rent, but most of the guys were contributing in some way. A couple of guys were just along for the ride, expecting everyone else to carry their weight. We were Christians, so we knew we needed to be gracious and patient. But there's a fine line between helping your brother in need and becoming your brother's doormat.

One day, I got home from a long day of work and opened the refrigerator to grab my dinner. I had been shopping the night before, and I discovered that while I was gone, Shawn had eaten all my food. Luckily, there's a Bible verse for everything, so I posted this one on the refrigerator door:

"If anyone is not willing to work, let him not eat" (2 Thessalonians 3:10).

It got the intended results. Shawn was out looking for a job the next day.

Confrontation can often feel like a spur in the side. What do you do when you see your brother sliding into sexual sin and compromising his values? Or when you know a friend is lying about something? Or when someone close to you begins to drift away from a life of seeking God? Do you spur him, or do you just pray a quiet prayer? This is where community gets messy. Because if you are both committed to discipleship—becoming more like Jesus—then you *need* to talk to him. You need to share your concerns.

When life brings confrontation, there are really only four options. The first option is you can let it *roll off* your back. Like water on a duck, you don't address it, you don't think about it, and you don't even let it bother you. You act like it never happened. This might be the most common response in Christian community, and while it seems gracious at first glance, this response at its root is cowardly. It will eventually erode trust and create distance in any friendship.

A second option is to *roll over* people like a tank on a battlefield. Whenever anyone makes a mistake, you address the problem right away, but when you're done, people don't feel loved—they feel like roadkill. This will also kill a healthy community, because everyone will walk around on eggshells, afraid of your wrath. Soon, this tactic will create more and more distance between friends.

The third option when confronted with conflict is to simply *roll out*. When things get tense, you get going. You leave the community, exit the group, or distance yourself from the friendship. You cut people out of your life when things get too personal, leading to a life of restarts and redos. Tragically, you will suffer most if you choose this option. Your life will never be deeply rooted, because when a seed is constantly dug up and replanted, it can't produce anything worthwhile.

There is a fourth option. We can learn to *roll up* our sleeves and address the problem lovingly and directly. Get into the mess. Dive into the problem. Don't hide. Don't steamroll. It's messy and time-consuming, but this is the *IDEAL* way to confront sin and offense:

- *Initiative*: Godly confrontation starts with initiative. Don't leave it alone or hope things change. Pray, but don't *just* pray. When we begin to feel a sense of obligation and responsibility for our friends in Jesus, we know that we are now entering the real body of Christ (Matthew 18:15).
- *Direct Communication*: Don't talk with other people about the person or their problems. Go directly to the source. Be honest. Be gracious, but be direct (Matthew 5:24).
- *Enter Humbly*: Don't assume you know the whole story, and don't act as though you are more worthy or righteous than your brother. We all come

to Jesus by grace alone. Always take ownership
for your mistakes and failures before you start
pointing out someone else's (Micah 6:8).

- *A Team Player*: Being a team player means that
rather than treating this person as your enemy,
you treat them as though you are on the same
team. Your goal is to strengthen them in their
pursuit of Jesus. Don't make confrontation a you-
against-them thing. Treat the other person like a
teammate (Romans 12:10).

- *Listener*: This might be the most important part
of godly confrontation. Before you accuse anyone of anything, and before you tell them all the
things that they did wrong, listen to their heart.
Hear their side of the story. Ask questions, and
take the time to really understand (James 1:19).

This simple framework can serve as an IDEAL way to approach
confrontation. It's never easy, but in the end honorable confrontation strengthens relationships. Jesus taught that whatever measure of
grace you use with others, that's the measure that God will use with
you (Matthew 7:1–5). And being a part of community means that
there will be times when people confront you about your sin. How
will you respond? Will you listen and learn, or will you just defend
yourself? Are you more interested in protecting your appearance or
becoming like Jesus?

Being this close with other people means that confrontation and
offense are unavoidable. How many times should you forgive? At
least 490 times (Matthew 18:21–22). In other words, you should

forgive so many times that it's impossible to accurately keep track. If you are willing to do that, the sharp edge of confrontation works more like a scalpel and less like a weapon. God uses your awkward, imperfect confrontations to knit your heart to others and deepen your love.

> We all come to Jesus by grace alone. Always take ownership for your mistakes and failures before you start pointing out someone else's.

Deeper Security

Being a part of a community that pursues God together and lovingly confronts one another is terrifying and exhilarating at the same time. It requires courage, humility, and a willingness to change. It requires a deep sense of inner security so that when you fail or let people down, you can bounce back and move forward together. But how do we cultivate an inner security like that?

In the midst of Paul's encouragement to live for the *upward call*, he gave us a glimpse into God's answer. "Not that I have already obtained this or am already perfect, but I press on to make it my own, *because Christ Jesus has made me his own*" (Philippians 3:12). I love Paul's posture toward the process of spiritual growth. He didn't pretend to have arrived. He didn't present himself as though he had figured everything out. Instead, he acknowledged that he was in process. This is stunning since Paul was maybe the greatest apostle to ever live. If he said that *he* was still in process, then we all should quickly acknowledge our need for continued growth.

Then Paul shared for us the driving force behind his life—the one truth that gave him the courage to stick with the process of discipleship: "I press on to make it my own, *because Christ Jesus has made me his own*" (Philippians 3:12). Paul's passion to know God was fueled by the truth that *God had a passion to know him!* Jesus made Paul his own. The literal translation of the word used is "apprehended." So, Christ apprehended Paul. Jesus ran him down, grabbed him, knocked him to the ground, and arrested him. God came looking for him and found him.

It wasn't Paul's wisdom or self-awareness that led to his salvation. He was saved because Jesus went out and found him, and that radical act of grace set Paul's heart on fire with gratitude and spiritual hunger. It provided stability and security even when he failed or didn't measure up. It provided a deep reservoir of acceptance.

And what was true of Paul is true for you. "For we know, brothers loved by God, that he has chosen you" (1 Thessalonians 1:4). The only way that you could say yes to Jesus in the first place is by the Spirit who drew you to him. God opened your eyes! No one can come unless the Father draws them (John 6:44). You are a disciple of Jesus because Jesus came and found you. Without his illuminating power in your heart, sin would have kept you in the dark forever (2 Corinthians 4:4). This means that the same stability and endurance that Paul had—you can have!

The more you trust in God's love for you, the more passion you will find to follow him. This deep assurance of his love provides a sense of security that enables you to handle the challenging moments of confrontation in community.

Imagine what life could look like if you joined hands with other Christians and really spurred one another on to love and good deeds. Imagine the depth of friendship and the power of accountability. Imagine the impact your community could have on the world around you.

But you don't just have to imagine it. You can live it. You can experience it for yourself. *Discipleship sets direction.*

— SACRED STEPS —

As you reflect on the content of this chapter, consider taking the following steps to grow:

1. Reflect on the implications of the compound effect your community has had on your spiritual growth. Think of one way you can intentionally spend time around fervent, focused followers of Jesus. Add one event to your calendar that will inspire or strengthen your passion for God.

2. Make a list of five other Christians in your life. Think of one way you can encourage each one of them like Jonathan encouraged David. Act on it this week.

3. For the next thirty days, practice a "daily examen" for the last five minutes before you go to sleep. Review each part of your day in your mind and ask yourself, "Where did I love others well today? Where did I fail to love others well?"

7

FUN AMPLIFIES GRACE

"If you're not allowed to laugh in heaven,
I don't want to go there."[49]

Martin Luther

"Clap along if you feel like a room without
a roof; because I'm happy."[50]

Pharrell Williams

"I do believe, in my heart, that there may be as much
holiness in a laugh as in a cry; and that, sometimes,
to laugh is the better thing of the two."[51]

Charles Spurgeon

"Everyone serves the good wine first ... But
you have kept the good wine until now."

John 2:10

It was Mike's first week of work, and I was so excited to have him on board. The church had grown significantly over the first year, and we had launched our second location thirteen months after starting our first. We had absolutely no idea what we were doing. Every Thursday, I would record my sermon in my friend Cheech's garage, and we would play the recording at our new Bridgeport location, twenty-five minutes away from where I was preaching live. We had no paid staff in Bridgeport. We had no real leadership structure. We had a few committed volunteers, a band, and a video—and yet somehow, in the kindness of God, this new church *grew*.

Therefore, of course, we were convinced our plan was foolproof.

It was only a few weeks into the launch of our Bridgeport location that it became obvious that we had bitten off far more than we could chew. Things were unraveling, and no one was there to lead. So, I started looking for the right person to hire on staff, and Mike turned out to be just the right guy.

Mike was our first full-time hire besides me at the church, and we had known each other from a distance through mutual friends. The interview process was a joke. We hung out a few times, I asked a couple of questions, then I offered him the job. When he said yes, I was as surprised as anyone. I wanted him to feel welcome the first week, so I came up with a small "welcoming" experience.

The night before Mike was supposed to start working for the church, I posted a picture of an adorable baby sheep on Craigslist with the caption "Free baby sheep. First come, first served. Call anytime, day or night." I then left Mike's cell phone number as the contact.

Mike stumbled into work the first day, noticeably tired. I was excited to have him there. "Hey, Mike, welcome to the staff! How's it going?" I asked.

"Uh, it's going *okay* … My phone rang all night with people asking me for my free baby sheep. I hardly slept. I think I'm trapped in some prank … My phone number must have gotten posted somewhere …"

I tried so hard to keep a serious look on my face and hold it in, but when I was belly laughing on the floor, it became pretty obvious that I knew something about this baby sheep mix-up.

He looked at me bewildered. "Wait. You?"

The story still makes me laugh today, all these years later. The look on his face—the subtle despair in his voice—*priceless*. I learned right away that Mike was the kind of guy who could take a joke, and he could also dish one out if he needed to.

When was the last time you had a good laugh, a laugh that reached down into your toes? When was the last time you were doubled over, unable to stop laughing? The Scripture teaches that a cheerful heart is good medicine (Proverbs 17:22). Laughter and fun will produce in the body a physical response that, in the long run, keeps you healthier. Scientists across various disciplines agree: "Laughter strengthens your immune system, boosts mood, diminishes pain, and protects you from the damaging effects of stress. Nothing works faster or more dependably to bring your mind and body back into balance than a good laugh."[52]

Your body was hardwired for fun.

Cheerfulness is one of the most contagious elements in human personality. Even the look on someone else's face can change the way you feel. "A cheerful look brings joy to the heart" (Proverbs 15:30 NLT). There really is something infectious about a smile. The more you are around happy people, the more it rubs off on you. And the happier you are, the happier you make others. One study found that "when an individual becomes happy, a friend living within a mile experiences a 25 percent increased chance of becoming happy."[53] You were hardwired for *fun*.

But this is where things get a little complicated. There's something deep inside all of us that resonates with the importance of laughter and lightheartedness, but so many of us live with such little fun. We don't laugh. We don't joke. We hardly even smile. What's wrong with us? Why do we struggle to really have fun? The answer may be more complicated than we think.

Broken Fun

Where do you go to really have a good time? When most people read that question, *church* is not the first answer that comes to mind. Think about your childhood. What images of fun are engraved on your memory? I remember as a kid spending time with my older cousin Billy. One night when my parents were gone, he walked down the stairs and proudly announced to my brother and me, "It's time to throw some snowballs at cars." Was that supposed to be fun?

We spent the night hiding out in the woods, bombing cars with balls of ice as they drove by. Drivers would pull over to the side of the road, furious as we scampered into our hiding places. One guy jumped out of his car after being pelted with an ice ball and tried to track us down, screaming and swearing the entire time. He never found us. When we finally reconvened, our adolescent hearts were pounding. That was dangerous. It was stupid. But was it ... fun?

The image of fun that we learn in our culture is often connected to hurtful behavior. We learn that it's fun to take something and not get caught. It's fun to sleep around and then quickly move on to the next relationship. It's fun to belittle someone with your quick wit or tell a dirty joke that makes everyone else blush. It's fun to mock others for their physical appearance. Fun in this context seems to cost someone else or put someone down. *Fun* has been connected to *bad*—so now being a little bad is kind of cool.

In shaping and defining fun, it seems the devil has dominated the market. His goal is to get you to commit to things for enjoyment that will eventually steal all your joy. Most of us don't even realize that we've been deceived about what real fun is, and we have surrendered the territory without a fight. We no longer believe that fun belongs to God, and far too often, Christians assume that if it's fun, it must be something God forbids. Followers of Jesus are often seen today as those who don't know how to have fun, and God is viewed as the invisible police officer, working overtime to ruin our fun.

What does *fun* mean to you? Have you given it any thought? Is fun always tied to entertainment? Is fun always connected to the weekend? Does it require a hobby you enjoy? If we are really hardwired for fun, then it's probably important for us to figure out what *fun* really means.

As you look out over our society, which is obsessed with having a little fun, do you see millions of people fulfilled and satisfied? Or has all our fun-seeking left us empty? Maybe we've been looking for fun in the wrong places. Proverbs teaches that "the lips of an immoral woman are as sweet as honey, and her mouth is smoother than oil. But in the end she is as bitter as poison, as dangerous as a double-edged sword" (Proverbs 5:3–4 NLT). "Stolen bread tastes sweet, but it turns to gravel in the mouth" (Proverbs 20:17 NLT).

No one wants to eat a sword or choke on gravel, and not all fun is created equal. Some fun costs us far more than we gain. That snarky comment you made to a friend felt witty at the time, but it hurt the person you aimed it at. Soon, there's a noticeable distance in your friendship and you wonder why. Was the fun worth it?

That tiny lie you told your spouse ends up coming to light and erodes trust in the relationship. It felt so small and harmless at the time. But now everything between the two of you seems to turn into an argument. Is that fun?

Going to a concert is fun. Watching a great movie is fun. Visiting Disney World is fun. Entertainment isn't all bad, but too often our fun requires lots of money and a stage with lights. We've shifted the responsibility of fun off ourselves and onto the entertainer. We don't make up games anymore. We don't sit around the campfire and tell stories. Rather than actually engaging with the people in our lives, we usually take the role of the passive observer. Turn on the TV, sit down on the couch next to a friend, and never say five meaningful words to each other. Is this *fun*?

Our attitude toward fun can often be summed up as *Show me what you got. Wow me. Impress me. If it's good, then I had fun.* Every concert needs to be better than the last one. Once you've been wowed a few times, you become a little harder to impress. Soon, our senses are numb, and we find ourselves always looking for something new.

The average American is stuffing himself with entertainment like a Thanksgiving turkey, yet at the same time, many of us find ourselves bored. We watch TV for hours and stay glued to our phones, all while we become less and less comfortable engaging in conversation with the people around us. What is the result of the entertainment fog all around us? It's turning out to be not nearly as fun as we thought it would be.

Is it possible that our inaccurate perception of fun is keeping us from having the fun that God intended? What is *real fun*? Where can we find it? And how do we live with more fun in our lives? To answer these questions, we must examine the assumptions we've made about God.

Happy Right Now

Beneath our cultural misunderstanding of fun is a deeper misunderstanding about God. Life is serious and we live in a world with real problems. There's poverty, brokenness, and pain. If you have been breathing for more than a few years, then you've already experienced your share of loss, betrayal, disappointment, and sorrow. In the midst of the trials and tragedies of life, it's often hard to have fun. How can we laugh in times like this? How can we smile? And where is God? Does he care? Does he see?

Because of the sin all around us and within us, it seems that many people struggle to imagine a God who is fun. We assume that he must be angry or at least disengaged. We assume that he either doesn't care about us or doesn't have the power to do anything about our problems. Surprisingly, Scripture paints a radically different picture of God. He *is* holy. He *does* bring wrath upon sin. He *is* all-powerful. But along with these qualities, the God who created all things is also *fun*.

When I was a kid, my dad used to take us every year to the zoo near our house. It was a tiny zoo, and my brother and I could see every exhibit in about thirty minutes. But we'd often stop and spend most of our time with the otters. The otter exhibit was small, and there were usually two or three little otters swimming around. They had a slide and a tunnel, and they didn't act like all the other animals. While the tigers spent their entire days sleeping in the corner, the otters were having a party. We'd lose track of time watching them play. They would fly down their slide, jump into the water, and chase one another around in circles.

> But along with these qualities, the God who created all things is also *fun*.

No one had to teach these animals to have fun. They were playful *by nature*. And their playfulness was intended to reveal something about God. "For since the creation of the world God's invisible qualities—his eternal power and divine nature—have been clearly seen, being understood from what has been made" (Romans 1:20 NIV). God made otters so that we could learn something about him. He's described in 1 Timothy 1:11 as the "happy God," and the prophet Jeremiah tells us that God "rejoices" in doing good to us (Jeremiah 32:41). God thinks it's fun to bless us! Right now, God is *happy*.

Does that idea bother you a little bit? Don't misunderstand: God's not happy about the pain in this world. He's not happy about sin. God can feel more than one thing at one time, and pain and sin grieve him deeply, but his overarching demeanor isn't worry, sorrow, or frustration. Remember the doctrine of the Trinity we explored in chapter 2? Independent of our sin or our success, God, within himself, is happy. Theologian Jonathan Edwards noted that "part of God's fullness which he communicates is his *happiness*. This happiness consists in enjoying and rejoicing in himself."[54]

God can be happy and holy at the same time. In fact, this is one of the great secrets of his nature. Holiness and happiness go together.

The holier you are, the happier you will be, and the happier you are, the holier you become.

Jesus revealed the heart of God throughout the Gospels and modeled for us God's holiness and happiness. In John chapter 21, Jesus met the disciples on the beach after his resurrection. The disciples had been fishing all night, and Peter and the others were exhausted. Jesus appeared in his resurrected body, but he did not immediately announce himself. Instead, he sauntered along on the shore and shouted out, "Children, do you have any fish?" (John 21:5). The disciples didn't immediately recognize him, so he performed a miracle to get their attention. When they arrived on the beach, he was already cooking breakfast.

This isn't the picture of the resurrected Jesus that we might imagine. He didn't show up with an entourage of angels. He didn't float in from outer space. Instead, he was casual. But there's something else to notice here. Jesus in this instance was *playful*.

In another resurrection account, Jesus met two disciples on the road to Emmaus, and again they didn't immediately recognize him. He asked what they were talking about, and they were surprised that he was unaware of what had been happening in Jerusalem (Luke 24:13–20). They walked and talked for a long time, and Jesus did not immediately reveal who he was. Finally, he opened their eyes and they recognized him, but as soon as they did, he disappeared. What was he up to? Once again, I'm pretty sure he was chuckling to himself. He was having fun. God has a sense of humor.

Sometimes we think of fun and laughter as something irreverent, and it certainly can be. But not all fun is irreverent. It's possible to laugh even in the midst of great sorrow. God's sense of humor does not mean that he lacks compassion or takes sin lightly. To understand happiness, playfulness, and laughter, we must understand that these emotions can live alongside sorrow and loss. When we see the goodness of God for what it really is, it doesn't instantly remove all our sorrows, but it does change them. We can learn to be sorrowful yet always rejoicing as we learn to see God as he truly is.

The God Who Laughs

The story of Abraham and Sarah reveals an aspect of God's nature that is essential to understanding his heart. God called this married couple to leave their home, and they obeyed and believed the promise that they would have a child. Abraham was over seventy years old when God made this promise, and Sarah wasn't far behind. They were way past the years of childbearing.

Even in their old age, God didn't bring the promise right away. Ten years passed, then another five—still no child. Finally, God visited the couple again and affirmed his promise. But at this point, Abraham was so old and they'd waited so long that the idea of having a baby felt ridiculous. "Then Abraham fell on his face and laughed" (Genesis 17:17). "Sarah was listening at the tent door.... So Sarah laughed to herself" (Genesis 18:10–12).

Abraham and Sarah couldn't hold in their laughter. But behind their chuckles and smiles were a host of emotions. What made them laugh? It was a collision of irony and awe, of unbelief and faith. It was the sheer ridiculousness of the thought that God would begin the lineage of salvation with a geriatric couple who had been unable to have children for seventy years.

And yet there was a strange sense that it was actually going to happen. They laughed because they had wanted to have children so badly for so long that the thought of it happening brought back to the surface all those years of disappointment. Hope had been deferred. Dreams had been delayed. But *now*? Could it be true? They had cried themselves to sleep so many nights. God told them that a baby was on the way and to name their miracle son Isaac, which means "laughter."

Frederick Buechner wrote, "At that moment when the angel told them they'd better start dipping into their old age pensions for cash to build a nursery, the reason they laughed was that it suddenly dawned on them that the wildest dreams they'd ever had hadn't been half wild enough."[55]

This story reveals something so important about God. It teaches us that in this life, there will be delays. There will be loss and sorrow and sadness. In this life, there will be times of mourning. But after time has expired—when it looks like God has failed and the promise never came—after the clock has run out—God will fulfill all that he has spoken. Nothing is hopeless. Nothing is ever truly lost. Your wildest dreams aren't half wild enough.

Buechner observed:

> God is the comic shepherd who gets more of a kick out of that one lost sheep once he finds it again than out of the ninety and nine who had the good sense not to get lost in the first place. God is the eccentric host who, when the country-club crowd all turned out to have other things more important to do than come live it up with him, goes out into the skid rows and soup kitchens and charity wards and brings home a freak show.[56]

God rarely ever does things the way we expect, and his plan to save us, heal us, and free us is no exception.

He is a happy God, and he has given us a reason to be happy too. Because while we were still sinners, Christ died for us. He came and found us, forgave us, redeemed us, adopted us, and plans to glorify us. He has given us the righteous standing of Jesus Christ. Now, because of the cross, we learn the unfathomable truth that God sees us through the light of his Son—and because of grace he is very happy with *you*.

Right with God

In John chapter 2, Jesus performed his first recorded miracle. We're told that this miracle served as one of his signs. A sign is something that points you somewhere, and that's exactly what Jesus was doing through this miracle. He was pointing us toward the heart of God, and it's important that Jesus decided to express it as his *first* sign. This was the first thing he wanted us to know about God.

> God rarely ever does things the way we expect, and his plan to save us, heal us, and free us is no exception.

The miracle took place at a wedding that Jesus and his new disciples were attending. In the culture of that time, weddings were massive celebrations, often lasting multiple days. Food was important, along with dancing and a host of other traditions. But maybe even more important was the wine. Wine was the symbol of celebration. The people were not there to get drunk; that would dishonor the family. But they took their wine very seriously, and it was the responsibility of the groom to ensure that there was plenty of wine for his guests.

At this particular wedding, the wine ran out, and Mary, the mother of Jesus, asked her son to intervene. If everyone at this wedding learned that the groom had failed at his responsibility, it would be a massive social embarrassment, and it would reflect very poorly on his ability to provide for his new family. When Mary asked Jesus to help, his response seemed cold and almost disrespectful: "Woman, what does this have to do with me?" (John 2:4). But Mary didn't seem to take offense at his words. Why not?

Reading Jesus' response might not clearly reveal his intent. What if Jesus said this with a sparkle in his eye or cracked a subtle smile as he spoke? What if his response wasn't cold or disrespectful at all, but playful? I imagine Jesus locking eyes with his mother and flashing her a grin. One theologian called his response *playful sparring*. Was Jesus, in this moment, having fun with his mom?

The next thing we know, Jesus asked some of the servants working at the wedding to fill six stone jars to the brim with water. These jars were used for the ceremonial washing practiced by the Jews. The washing was not an attempt at good hygiene. It was a reminder of sin. Jews were expected to wash at various times as a constant acknowledgment to God of their own unclean position before him. It was an act of humility to affirm their unworthiness. Humans are sinful. God is holy—so the Jews would wash.

Once the jars were full of water, Jesus instructed the servants to bring the water to the master of the feast. He tasted the water, which had now become wine, and he immediately found the groom. And he said to the groom, "Everyone serves the good wine first, and when people have drunk freely, then the poor wine. But you have kept the good wine until now" (John 2:10).

There's something obvious about this miracle that's worth noting. Jesus made *wine* at a *party*. That alone might rattle your cage. Jesus was a lot of *fun*. He was social, and he wasn't shy about celebration. He loved a good party, he who displayed for us the exact imprint of God's nature (Hebrews 1:3). Of course, he wasn't endorsing drunkenness, but his miracle was extravagant—over 150 gallons of very good wine! The bride and groom were probably drinking that wine for decades!

But there is more to this miracle, and that's why we are told that it was a sign. It's intended to serve as an allegory, a picture of what Jesus came to do for everyone. Sin began with Adam, the first man, who did not protect his bride from the serpent and who gave in to temptation. Adam proved to be a poor provider for his new family.

Through the sin that Adam committed, sin now lives in us. So, in God's view, *Adam* lives in us. His sin has become ours by nature and by choice, and it still sabotages our relationship with God. But Jesus came to undo the work of sin and reverse the curse of Adam. He became a "second Adam" to represent us before God. He filled up the requirement of righteousness given in the moral law. He filled it to the brim, just as the water jars were filled.

But then he exchanged places with us on the cross, and he took our sin (which created the need for us to be made clean) and turned it into wine (the symbol of celebration). Notice in the story that when the unprepared groom was praised for the wine, Jesus didn't take the credit. The groom got all the credit when he deserved all the shame. Jesus did the work, and the undeserving man got the glory! And this is the story of grace. You are the unprepared groom. You deserve shame, but Jesus gives you his wine instead.

It's important to see that the groom did not reject the gift. He didn't demand an explanation of where it came from. Instead, he humbly received the credit for something he had not earned.

This story is intended to teach us the secret of grace. The only way to experience the inner celebration of grace is to abandon your compulsion to earn it. Once freely received, the good news of God's grace fundamentally changes your heart, just as the news of the wine changed the wedding. You move from striving to peace, from desperation to joy, and from hopelessness to celebration. God's gift through Jesus often feels like an *uncomfortable abundance*. But accepting his gift fully and freely will cause your heart to laugh like Abraham and Sarah. It's so ridiculous. It's so impossible—it's too good *not* to be true.

Of course, this doesn't mean that life isn't serious. There will still be sorrow, loss, and pain. But when the eternal truth of the gospel sinks deeper and deeper in your heart, sorrow looks different. We can rest in the providential plan of God even as we live in a world that feels out of control. We can trust God's timing in everything, even when it looks like it's too late and the door has closed. We can stop blaming God for all the pain in this world, knowing that it comes from sin and the devil and knowing that in the end God will triumph over sorrow.

Rather than immediately removing every trial, God has chosen to redeem the trials through his secret orchestration of all things. Like Joseph learned after being betrayed by his brothers and sold into slavery, "You intended to harm me, but God intended it for good to accomplish what is now being done, the saving of many lives" (Genesis 50:20 NIV).

In his inexhaustible wisdom, God is working everything for his glory and the good of his children. Sometimes this is hard to believe. But God will prove his promise again and again until our hearts find rest. So, it's not irreverent to laugh. It's not irreverent to dance, even when life is a mess. Often, laughter is the holiest response of all.

Gospel Fun

What kind of life should the good news of God's grace produce among us? Certainly, we should take our pursuit of God very seriously. Like an Olympic athlete or a disciplined military officer, Christians should give themselves fully to the eternal purpose of Jesus on the earth.

But even as we take God seriously, we shouldn't take ourselves too seriously, because the gospel reveals who we really are. We are a collision of weakness and glory—brokenness and beauty. Without Jesus, we are all a mess. But because of grace, we no longer need to pretend that we can hold ourselves together. So, we must learn to laugh at ourselves. We must learn to be lighthearted even as we are sober-minded. This is the beginning of true, holy *fun*.

Fun is not just about being entertained, and it doesn't have to come at the expense of others. Fun is simply the full enjoyment of the moment and a full heart that engages in playfulness. Are you able to laugh at yourself, or are you always caught up in keeping the right appearance? When we can chuckle at our own ridiculousness, it's a sign that the gospel is making headway in our hearts.

I remember years ago when God started teaching me about not taking myself so seriously. I was leading a traveling ministry, and we had just finished up an event. I preached that night, and I received an overwhelmingly positive response. People were buzzing about the amazing things I had shared and how insightful I was. I left the event feeling pretty good about myself. God had used me in a big way. I finished shaking hands and kissing babies and got into my friends' car to drive home.

> We must learn to laugh at ourselves. We must learn to be lighthearted even as we are sober-minded. This is the beginning of true, holy *fun*.

As we pulled out of the parking lot, my stomach started turning over. Maybe I ate something that bothered me. I hadn't felt sick minutes earlier. We merged onto the highway, but the traffic was at a complete stop. The next exit was miles away … and things started moving in my bowels that didn't feel natural. I needed a bathroom.

After about ten minutes of squirming, I realized I was never going to make it. I needed to go *now*, and my options were very limited. I opened my friend's glove box and found a stack of napkins. I turned to the two other people in the car and said, *"I'm sorry, guys, I've got to go!"*

Because of the traffic, the car was already stopped, so I opened the door and ran to the nearby woods off the highway. It was autumn in New England, and most of the leaves had already fallen off the trees. I reached what I hoped was an appropriately wooded area and realized that I could go no farther. I took two more steps and walked right into a small stream that I hadn't noticed in the dark. Standing in four inches of water, I squatted down. There was no bathroom for miles, so this wooded area would have to do.

And that's when I heard it. Honking.

It wasn't just from one car. It was dozens of different car horns, along with people whooping and hollering. I slowly turned my body and realized that, standing in this tiny stream, my backside was in full view of every stopped car on the highway. People were rolling down their windows to congratulate me. They honked and whooped for what felt like forever, and there was nothing I could do. I squatted there, frozen in time—free entertainment for a large highway audience.

I finished up as best I could, my emotions having swung from one extreme to another. Ten minutes earlier, I was walking tall, feeling like the greatest man of God in history. Now I sheepishly made my way back to the car, mortified and embarrassed. As I opened the door with my shoes soaking wet and my pant legs dripping from the stream, I had a split second to decide my response. Would I burst into tears? A big part of me wanted to. Would I try to play it cool and say nothing? It seemed like that option was off the table.

I got back into the car and sat down in the passenger seat. No one said a word. There were about eight long seconds of uncomfortable silence. And then the three of us in the car started uncontrollably laughing. I can remember the gut-busting feeling of soggy shoes and hilarious humiliation. It was just plain funny, and I needed to get over myself and laugh.

That night served as a sort of turning point for me. I decided that I didn't want to spend my life propping myself up and protecting my reputation. I wanted to make much of Jesus, and when my own frailty and foolishness were exposed, rather than running away from it all, I wanted to learn to lean into it. I still want to be the type of person who can laugh at himself, and not just chuckle, but really laugh. And I want to learn to poke fun at others in a way that doesn't discourage or hurt them but reveals my affection for them.

My good friend Cheech likes to say, "Embarrassment is a choice," and those words are packed with wisdom. No one is forcing you to be self-conscious. No one is making you obsess over what others think. You can be free, and that's the real power of grace. Because you are loved and accepted by God, you don't need to be so careful with appearances. You can be free, and you can even chuckle at your own imperfections.

What if we could form a community that was serious about holiness *and* serious about fun? What if we could become people who laughed often, were slow to take offense, and were unwilling to hold a grudge? What if our community was quick to forgive, quick to acknowledge the sheer silliness that often comes with life, and slow to protect our own reputation? A community like this would serve as a loudspeaker broadcasting a different message to a world that is consumed with appearances and approval.

This leads us to the fourth principle of biblical community: *fun amplifies grace.*

In other words, fun puts grace on display. It makes grace look beautiful and big and worth pursuing. The heart-change caused by the grace of God is displayed best through people who carry a profound sense of happiness. It can't be contrived or forced. It must flow out of real experience. But when grace gets in you, joy naturally comes out. And a life lived with a heart full of grace leads to relationships that are far more fun than anything this world can offer. *Fun amplifies grace.*

Enjoying Life

Did you know that God wants you to enjoy life? The Bible makes it clear that God treats us as his children and "richly provides us with everything for *our enjoyment*" (1 Timothy 6:17 NIV). He is a good Father, and he takes great pleasure in watching his kids enjoy his gifts. Why did he give us waves to play in at the beach? Why did he give us golden retrievers who live to chase their tails? Why did he give us delicious food and friends and sunsets? God gave us these things to enjoy, and it grieves his heart when his children don't stop to enjoy the gifts he's given.

The danger comes when we start to value the gifts over the Giver. God creates boundaries for our own good, and to ignore these boundaries is to dishonor God and to open ourselves up to painful consequences. But when we learn God's boundaries, we can enjoy God's gifts without idolizing them. "So whether you eat or drink or whatever you do, do it all *for the glory* of God" (1 Corinthians 10:31 NIV). God is glorified when we learn to celebrate his grace by enjoying his gifts.

Too often, we miss out on the fun God intended because we haven't learned to slow down and enjoy it. We chew our food too quickly, ignore the amazing flavors or the stunning sunrise outside the window, and walk past our kids to get out the door for work without saying a word. But this way of living doesn't honor God. When we take ourselves so seriously that we end up blowing past the people God has put in our lives, we display an image of God to the world that is out of step with his nature.

Christians should know how to have a good time better than anyone. We should invest in deep relationships, delight in the gifts all around us, and be quick to laugh at all the hilarious moments that life provides. All of this fun amplifies grace. C. S. Lewis expressed this idea powerfully when he wrote, "This does not mean that we are to be perpetually solemn. We must play. But our merriment must be of that kind (and it is, in fact, the merriest kind) which exists between people who have, from the outset, taken each other seriously."[57] Serious fun—that's what the *sacred us* is called to be.

A couple of years ago I studied the topic of joy in the Bible for twelve months. I went from the beginning of Scripture to the end, analyzing every verse about joy, trying to suck the marrow out of each sentence. I learned a lot through that study, but one thing in particular surprised me. As I went from passage to passage, I noticed how many times joy was connected to *others*. For some reason, I've always thought of joy as a very personal experience. But it turns out that joy can't be disconnected from relationship.

Scripture overflows with examples. "For I have derived much joy and comfort from your love" (Philemon 1:7). "For what is our hope or joy or crown ... Is it not you?" (1 Thessalonians 2:19). "I long to see you, that I may be filled with joy" (2 Timothy 1:4). "Complete my joy by being of the same mind, having the same love" (Philippians 2:2).

Verse after verse, I was confronted with the same idea: God intends joy to be a *community experience*. He wants you to learn to enter into the joy of others, and doing this causes your joy to overflow. When we intentionally invest in shared experiences and learn to not take ourselves so seriously, laughter and joy will find their own opportunities, and a new kind of community will form. Jesus gave us a sign when he turned the water into wine. Maybe we need to learn to celebrate a little more often. Maybe we need to smile a little more often. What would your Christian community look like if fun became a priority? *Fun amplifies grace.*

— SACRED STEPS —

As you reflect on the content of this chapter, consider taking the following steps to grow:

1. Take time to journal about three or four times in your life when you've felt embarrassed. Ask God to reveal insecurities in your heart and heal them with the truth of the gospel. Invite God to teach you to overcome embarrassment and the need to impress others through the power of his acceptance.

2. Share with a friend the parts of this chapter that stood out to you. Discuss together what it means to you to see God as *happy*.

3. Plan a get-together with two or three Christian friends. Don't just spend the night watching entertainment. Enjoy the gift of time together. Play a game, eat a great meal, and swap stories. When the get-together is over, journal about what God taught you and what you learned about fun.

8

MISSION DRIVES ADVENTURE

"If you can't fly, run; if you can't run, walk; if you can't walk, crawl; but by all means keep moving."[58]

Martin Luther King Jr.

"As you love God and serve Him, you will undoubtedly experience the greatest adventure life has to offer."[59]

Bill Bright

"I love to do new things."[60]

Bo Jackson

"And he who was seated on the throne said, 'Behold, I am making all things new.'"

Revelation 21:5

Four men standing at the top of a 6,093-foot-deep hole. In the middle of an incredibly busy time of ministry, three of the leaders in our church and I decided to get away for a few days, reflect on the past, and get on the same page about the future. We also decided to walk to the bottom of the Grand Canyon and back ... in a day. For seasoned hikers, this may not be that big a deal, but for *me*—a guy who really isn't into hiking or running—this eighteen-mile, nine-hour hike was a bit ambitious.

Things started out great as we left the parking area and began our descent. The sun was rising, the sky was clear, and the view of the canyon was breathtaking. We stopped and took pictures, making time to laugh and goof around. About two hours into our hike, we came to a large sign on the side of the path. It had a picture of a man throwing up and it read, "Hiking to the Colorado River and back in one day is not recommended ... If you think you have the fitness and expertise to attempt this extremely strenuous hike, please seek advice from a park ranger."

We hadn't talked to any park ranger, and I didn't think I had the fitness or the expertise. I read the sign out loud, then asked the guys I was with, "Hey, guys, wait a minute. Where are we hiking to?"

"The Colorado River and back," they answered.

By the time we had reached the bottom of the canyon, I started to realize the gravity of our choices. This was going to be grueling.

We began our ascent to the rim, and pretty soon, none of us were laughing or taking pictures. We started feeling less like friends on a hike and more like packhorses. Conversation came to a halt. The only sound was the crunching of the earth beneath our sneakers. When the water and snacks ran out, all that was left was the grind.

Take one more step. Take another. One more. I stopped looking at the beautiful ridges and snow-covered mountains. I stopped
searching for a glimpse of wildlife in the distance. Fifteen hours in,
I was almost exclusively looking at my feet, every once in a while
lifting my eyes to catch a glimpse of the rim of the canyon. That's
where we were headed, but sometimes an hour would go by and the
rim wouldn't look any closer.

In the final two hours of the hike, that rim became my sole
focus. I locked in and put all the energy I had left into reaching it.
One more step. One more. That rim became my *telos*. *Telos* is a Greek
word used by ancient philosophers to describe your end goal, your
destination, your bigger purpose. It's the place you shoot for at the
end of your hike. Without a telos in life, the human spirit can't continue to advance. But if you can keep the telos in your sights, you'll
often surprise yourself and find the strength to take another step.

When we got to the top of the Grand Canyon, we had nothing left. I looked around at the other guys with swollen feet and
exhausted faces. I don't really enjoy a normal hike, let alone a mega-
hike. As we sat on the floor of the nearby lodge and started making
fun of one another, an unexpected thought entered my mind. *That
was absolutely terrible ... and kind of awesome. I think I would probably do it again.*

In the story of creation, God commanded humanity to subdue
the earth (Genesis 1:28). It seems that since the days of Adam, this
primal call still lies dormant in the heart of every person. From the
very beginning of recorded history, the human race has been climb-
ing mountains, building towers, and exploring oceans, if for no other
reason than to simply subdue the earth.

Curiosity pushes us to know what is out there. We want to reach the top, walk around, and then come back again. We want to see what lives in that deep cave and what the view is like thirty thousand feet off the ground. It's why we still know the name Marco Polo and most of us have heard of Lewis and Clark.

Hardwired into the human psyche is an ache for exploration and adventure. And adventure makes things that are otherwise grueling become exciting. Walt Disney said it best: "We keep moving forward—opening up new doors and doing new things—because we're curious. And curiosity keeps leading us down new paths."[61]

Our problem is that we often lack a telos. We hunger for adventure, but we aren't entirely sure which expedition to take. We don't have a clear mission to accomplish, so we find ourselves seeking adventure simply for adventure's sake. Every year, Americans spend millions of dollars to experience a thrill. We go to amusement parks, travel to exotic places, and attempt challenging feats with the hope of capturing a few moments of adventure. Some people go even further, jumping out of airplanes or playing extreme sports. These adventures aren't bad or evil in themselves, but they don't seem to be enough. Adventure without telos—without a sense of a greater mission—ends up being hollow.

> You are an eternal being, and nothing short of an eternal mission will do.

Have you noticed how everyone seems to be searching for a cause? Our culture has created a buffet of options. Some people put all their energy around a political mission, believing that the advancement of a certain program or politician will save the world. Others put their weight behind a humanitarian cause. They are passionate about building wells in third-world countries or bringing shoes to impoverished kids. Some animal lovers make a certain endangered species the focus of their mission. They live to save the whales.

Is there anything wrong with being passionate about politics or saving the whales from extinction? Of course not. But these things can't be the highest rim in the hike of your life. If they are, you will soon discover that they will always leave you wanting, because your telos must stretch beyond this world and into the next. You are an eternal being, and nothing short of an eternal mission will do.

Tragically, few Christians live each day with an awe-inspired sense of the grand mission of God. If we're honest, we are often most passionate about our kids, our careers, or our vacations. Followers of Jesus before our time stated the real telos of life directly: "Man's chief end is to glorify God and enjoy him forever." We know that all things exist for God's glory. But in order for God's glory to be displayed in your life, you must understand, prioritize, and engage in God's *mission*. So, what exactly *is* God's mission?

All Things New

The story of life on earth begins with creation. In the beginning, God created both the visible and invisible world. He made humanity in his image and gave us dominion over the earth. But relationship with God was severed through our rebellion, and soon, sin and Satan tainted all that God had made. This led to God's great intervention and His incredible act of redemption through Jesus Christ.

Creation, fall, redemption is known by theologians as the meta-narrative or the bigger story of the Scripture. But there's a fourth component to the story that is often overlooked: *the restoration of all things*. It has always been God's plan to restore everything. In the book of Revelation, the apostle John gave us a glimpse of the final restoration.

> Then I saw a new heaven and a new earth, for the first heaven and the first earth had passed away, and the sea was no more. And I saw the holy city, new Jerusalem, coming down out of heaven from God, prepared as a bride adorned for her husband. And I heard a loud voice from the throne saying, "Behold, the dwelling place of God is with man. He will dwell with them, and they will be his people, and God himself will be with them as their God. He will wipe away every tear from their eyes, and death shall be no more, neither shall there be mourning, nor crying, nor pain anymore, for the former things have passed away."
>
> And he who was seated on the throne said, "Behold, I am making *all things new*." (Revelation 21:1–5)

This is the rim of the canyon, the climax in the story of life. This is the ultimate telos—God's plan to restore all things, making everything beautiful. But far too often, Christians have misinterpreted this text and not recognized the relevance it has for today. Jesus did not say, "Behold, *one day* I will make all things new." He said that the restoration of all things has already begun. We are not simply waiting for a future redemption. We are right now living in a present, active, moment of redemption.

In the New Testament, Jesus' resurrected body is called the firstfruits of the restoration of all things (1 Corinthians 15:20, 23; Colossians 1:18; Revelation 1:5). The firstfruits of any harvest are the first installment. They are the crops that matured earlier than the rest, and they mark the beginning of the harvest season. This language is intended to teach us that with the resurrection of Jesus, the plan of God to restore *everything* has officially begun.

Jesus told the religious leaders, "Truly, truly, I say to you, an hour is coming, and *is now here*, when the dead will hear the voice of the Son of God, and those who hear will live" (John 5:25). The hour has arrived. The door has now opened. The clock has started. And the restoration of all things has officially begun.

But how, according to this verse, are the dead raised? Jesus gives us the answer: they hear *his voice*. Theologians call this the doctrine of regeneration. Regeneration is the work of the Holy Spirit in granting spiritual life to sinners so that they are able to repent and trust in Christ, becoming a new creation. God opens our eyes. God awakens our spirit. And God gets all the glory.

This miracle of regeneration is one of the greatest wonders in the plan of God. And it's not just a future possibility. It's happening all around us right now. The restoration of all things has already begun.

We are presently living in the overlap of the kingdom of God and the kingdom of this world. In this present age, *both* kingdoms exist, but like a seed in the earth, the kingdom of God is already sprouting and expanding. Jesus described the reality of this overlap to his disciples when he told them, "There will be more rejoicing in heaven over one sinner who repents than over ninety-nine righteous persons who do not need to repent" (Luke 15:7 NIV). He wants us to know that heaven and earth are linked and that the things we do here have repercussions there.

God has put things in motion. He is already accomplishing his ultimate mission, and you and I are not just spectators in his plan to make all things new. He wants to draw our attention upward, to catch a glimpse of the rim and then participate in his eternal mission.

A Sacred Trust

A few months before writing this, I went on a five-day fly-fishing trip in Montana with a small group of pastors from all over the country. I had never been fly-fishing before, so my fishing expectations were pretty low going into the trip. One night, after a day of fishing, I found myself around a campfire with a couple of the other guys. Then one by one, every guy left, and it was just me and Dale.

I'd met Dale when I'd arrived at the lodge three days earlier. He's about twenty years older than me, and he's a pastor on staff with one of the largest churches in the country. Dale has watched their congregation grow from hundreds of people to tens of thousands over the last few decades. We sat out that night in the cold, huddled close to the fire, and I listened as Dale shared from the deepest part of his life.

He was grateful for all the growth the church had experienced. He understood the importance of good systems, strong church government, and financial accountability. He was good at these things. But none of these things were on Dale's heart. As the light from the fire bounced off his face, Dale shared what burned most deeply in him.

"People, Justin. There are so many people … And they're lost, Justin. Lost without God. We need to do more. We need to do something more … There are people and they don't know God and they're dying."

His words hung in the air. I could hear the trembling in his voice and feel the churning going on inside him. *People.* It was so simple, and so powerful. That night, I could hear the burning heart of God pulsating through the lives of his children.

What drove the Son of God to be made flesh? What compelled him toward the cross? What made his agony worth it, and what inspired him to walk out of the tomb? *People. They're lost without God. We need to do more. We need to do something more …*

Do you hear that call in your heart? God is calling you to actively participate in his mission to make all things new by becoming his voice on earth for people to hear and be made alive. This mission *is* the adventure of your life, and it has the power to set your heart on fire.

How valuable is one life? How valuable is one human soul? In our world, we often get tangled up in collecting new toys and new programs. We focus on our careers or our hobbies. We tinker with that classic car in the garage or become obsessed with that sports team or our home decor.

> This mission *is* the adventure of your life, and it has the power to set your heart on fire.

Don't feel bad about enjoying these things. They are all gifts from God. But they cannot serve as the driving force behind your life. You need more than a great job and a well-funded retirement.

God has called you to impact the eternal destiny of *people*—and until you are consistently participating in this great work, your life will lack a deep sense of purpose.

"What good is it," Jesus asked, "for someone to gain the whole world, yet forfeit their soul?" (Mark 8:36 NIV). Notice the implications of this statement. It means that one human soul is worth more than all the treasure of the world put together. This truth should bring a profound clarity to life. The plan of God to restore all things requires your participation. You are a part of his plan. "That is, in Christ God was reconciling the world to himself, not counting their trespasses against them, and *entrusting to us* the message of reconciliation" (2 Corinthians 5:19).

You have been given a sacred trust, and you have been called to fulfill a unique aspect of his plan to restore all things. You were not created to simply work a job, buy a nice house, raise your kids, and die. You were created to participate in the mission. "You are the salt of the earth…. You are the light of the world" (Matthew 5:13–14).

The primary use of salt at that time was to reverse the process of decay. It would be sprinkled on meats to stop bacteria from growing. In the same way, God sprinkles his people throughout the earth. Some are high school teachers, some are computer programmers, some are stay-at-home moms, some work on construction sites, some are truck drivers, some are stockbrokers. God sprinkles his people across the globe, calling every one of us to reverse the process of decay in our sphere of influence.

Sin, pride, lust, greed, fear, and shame grow like bacteria in every corner of the world. It's your job to be salt and light—to change the environment around you so that the Spirit of Jesus can make all things new. Are you starting to see the rim of the canyon? You have a telos. God has given you a great mission.

But in order to participate in the mission of God, he must rewire your values. The compassion of Jesus must disrupt your life to such a degree that you begin to really care about people like he does. Have you experienced an inner change like that?

Years ago, I read the biography of William Booth, the founder of the Salvation Army. God used Booth in a powerful way in his generation, leading countless thousands to faith in Christ. As I read his story, I was struck by his deep, fervent love for people. People were his obsession. They were his telos.

One story from Booth's life accurately summed up his passion. The year was 1910, and thousands of Salvation Army missionaries had gathered for their annual Christmas convention. Booth was supposed to give the keynote speech at the convention, but he became so sick the day before that he was unable to get out of bed. So instead of going to speak, he wrote a telegram to be read to the expectant crowd. With thousands of people gathered, William Booth's telegram was opened and read aloud. It surprisingly contained only one word: *Others.*[62]

That was it. That was the mission. And that was the story of his life. If you can understand that, then you've captured the heart of God.

The Greatest Thrill

Have you ever had the privilege of leading someone to Jesus? Have you ever taken the hand of another person and prayed with them as they turned their life over to Christ? Consider what's happening in heaven as you are praying. Angels are dancing. Believers who have gone before us are singing. God is leading the parade, and the joy is beyond expression. His child has come home, and they will live in the house of God forever. Heaven and earth work together in an eternal transaction.

There is no thrill like the thrill of an awakened heart. What will God do through this one? Only time will tell. Maybe she will lead a great ministry, rescuing girls from sex trafficking. Maybe she will raise two godly kids who will change the world after she's gone. No one knows exactly how God will write the story, but every story is sacred, and every soul carries immeasurable value.

A few years ago, in the lobby of our church, I had the privilege of praying with Matt as he turned his life over to Jesus. His story is like all our stories—full of unexpected twists and turns. Matt battled with drug addiction early in life and ended up far from home, living at a local rehab program near our church. But God had marked out his days and ordered his steps.

Today, years later, Matt is an amazing man of God. He met his wife at our church, started a business, and bought a house. He and his wife live with four other Christians and are walking out their own journey of intentional community. God uses Matt to lead others to Jesus constantly, and my heart sings every time I see God's power in his life. I know *I* didn't save Matt. I just had the privilege of praying with him that day. God did all the work. But I get to experience the joy of participating in one small turn in his story—and that joy is *incredible*.

When God intervenes and changes a life, the transformation of that one person echoes through countless other relationships. One of the greatest thrills in life is to watch the reverberations of a changed heart on a family tree. A few years ago, I met Javier at one of our church services. He was at a very low place, and he desperately wanted to open his life to God. I prayed with him that day, and Javier fully surrendered his life to Jesus.

It wasn't until weeks later that I began to learn Javier's story. He and his wife were separated, and Javier was on the verge of walking away from his family. His two kids hardly saw their dad. He was searching for God, but the situation looked hopeless. One day, the darkness around him had become so consuming that he lost all hope and decided to take his own life. He hung a belt from the rafters of the room and wrapped it around his neck. As he hung there, expecting this to be the end, the belt snapped.

Somehow, God had intervened. God had spared his life. Javier didn't know what was next, but when his wife told him about a church she had been attending, he was open to come and see. We met on his first day at church. He invited Jesus into his life, and soon, everything started to change. His marriage was restored. His family came back together. God worked a great miracle. Now, years later, our kids are friends, and God is using Javier and his family in amazing ways to reach others.

A few months ago, I stood back and watched his son Joe play with my son Ezra. They were laughing and pretending, lost in the world of imagination of seven-year-old boys. Seemingly out of nowhere, I started crying.

As tears ran down my face, I found myself overwhelmed by the reality that *God really does change family trees*. I already knew that, but every time I see it, the truth takes my breath away. God rewrites the history of families.

What if that belt hadn't snapped? What if that attempt at suicide hadn't failed? The little boy in front of me wouldn't have a daddy.

But today he does have a daddy. And his dad is on the sidelines of all his football games. He's teaching him how to ride a bike without training wheels and how to throw a football. Joe has a dad who, most importantly, is teaching him about Jesus, and his entire life will look different because God is in the process of making all things new.

The experience reminded me of what Dale had said, sitting around that campfire on our fly-fishing trip.

People. It's about people, Justin. They're lost without God. We need to do more …

You don't have to be a preacher to make an impact. God has placed everyone somewhere for a purpose, and all around you, there are people in need of him. You don't need a PhD in evangelism. You don't need a perfect presentation of biblical theology. Instead, you simply need to be yourself, share your story, and stay available. God gives every one of us different gifts, and that's part of what makes his mission so exciting.

You might have the gift of hospitality. You can't preach a sermon, but you can cook dinner. Inviting your neighbors over for a cookout could be the door that leads to a transformed life.

You might be skilled in business, and rather than taking that extra vacation, you choose to give that money to finish the building project at the church. Your money paid for the seats in the auditorium, where a single mom at the end of her rope walked in, sat down, and encountered God. That seat wouldn't have been there if it wasn't for you. But you leveraged your gift for an eternal mission, and you get the thrill of watching God's kingdom advance through your sacrifice.

Are you starting to see how it's all connected? The deep thirst for adventure that lives in all of us must be aimed at an eternal mission.

And this is where we find the fifth principle of biblical community. You were created for adventure, and your heart will never be fully alive until you're living the adventure every day. The thirst for adventure can't be satisfied with trips to the Caribbean or a fancy new car, because you were created for an eternal purpose—to participate in the mission of God. You are called to reverse the process of decay and, with Jesus, make all things new. When you are fully engaged in that mission, you will be fully alive.

And the mission takes all of us. We learn together, advance together, and celebrate together. This is the fifth principle of biblical community: *mission drives adventure*.

Creatively Compelled

How far will you go to advance the mission of Jesus? What will you do to impact your sphere of influence? Will you reorganize your schedule? Will you restructure your spending? If the mission of Jesus does not disrupt your life in some way, then you won't experience any sense of adventure. It only becomes an adventure when it involves a certain degree of risk. Mission must become aggressive. It must become personal. It must become *creative*.

Years ago, just after we started our first church, our small group of volunteers were brainstorming creative ways to introduce people to Jesus. Someone on the team had heard the news that the '90s hip-hop group Salt-N-Pepa were performing a free concert on the downtown green. I hadn't heard anything from Salt-N-Pepa since I was a little kid. It was in that moment that I had a stupid idea. I looked at my friend Nick and asked, "Do we still have those extra flyers inviting people to the church?"

"Yeah," he said. "We've got tons of them."

"I just had an idea," I told him. "Grab the Elmo suit."

Our church had purchased an Elmo suit for a kids' event earlier that summer, and that costume seemed to carry a certain magnetic power. When Elmo showed up at the event, everyone wanted a picture. People didn't want to come say hello to Justin, but they were more than willing to accept an invitation from Elmo. So, Nick and I took a backpack full of church invites and an Elmo suit down to the New Haven Green, where thousands of people had shown up with their lawn chairs to hear Salt-N-Pepa.

> If the mission of Jesus does not disrupt your life in some way, then you won't experience any sense of adventure. It only becomes an adventure when it involves a certain degree of risk.

Elmo stole the show that night as huge crowds gathered to take pictures and say hello, and we handed out every flyer we had. I'll never forget the crowds of people dancing with Elmo as Salt-N-Pepa performed in the background. It was a hilarious moment that we still laugh about today. But what were we thinking? Who goes to the downtown green on a Saturday night with Elmo to invite people to church? I guess we do. Because love for people will always creatively compel you beyond your routines and comforts.

What's holding you back from creatively using your weekend to make an impact for God? Who has God brought into your life? What windows of opportunity can you open? There really is an adventure waiting for you, but it won't be neat and tidy. It will be messy. It will be costly. And it won't always be safe.

Safety is a fundamental desire for all of us, especially in the West, and it seems in recent years to be gathering more fans than ever. The world around us is a dangerous place, and we want our homes to be safe, our cars to be safe, and our kids to be safe. There is nothing wrong with wanting to be safe, but our focus on safety can cause us to forfeit the mission of God. Safety cannot become a prerequisite for obedience. Sometimes it seems that we pray conditional prayers.

"God, I'll do anything to serve you. My life belongs to you. I give you my heart fully. Lead me wherever you want to take me ... as long as it's safe."

What happens when things go wrong? What happens when the mission gets messy? A few years ago, two friends and I stopped on the highway to help someone whose car had broken down. John and I pushed the broken car off the highway, while Jeremiah waited in our car in the breakdown lane.

It was late at night when another driver came up over the hill. The driver had drifted into the breakdown lane and hit our car going seventy miles an hour. My friend Jeremiah spent a month in the hospital with eleven broken bones. All because we had stopped to help someone in need. After that accident, I didn't stop to help another person on the side of the road for years. Every time I was presented with the opportunity to help, I hesitated, then drove past the stopped car. "Someone else will stop," I told myself. It just didn't feel safe.

The uncomfortable truth that we tend to avoid is that *following Jesus isn't safe*. It never has been, and Jesus never promised that it would be. It will cost you, and the cost will look different for each of us. It might cost you your comfort or your popularity. It might feel like an interruption or a conflict with your personal priorities. Following Jesus could even cost you your life.

But isn't there more to life than simply breathing? Life only makes sense when it's lived for eternity, and life without adventure isn't life at all. Helen Keller wrote, "Security is mostly a superstition. It does not exist in nature, nor do the children of men as a whole experience it. Avoiding danger is no safer in the long run than outright exposure. Life is either a daring adventure, or nothing."[63]

Which phrase more accurately describes your life? Is it more like a *daring adventure* or *nothing*? What's stopping you from living a life on mission? What's stopping you from living a better story?

A Better Story

Every summer our family makes the trip from New Haven, Connecticut, to St. Augustine, Florida. Chrisy's family lives in St. Augustine, and since we have four kids and a dog, it often makes more sense to drive to Florida rather than fly. Sometimes my wife and daughter will fly down while the three boys and I make the nineteen-hour drive in the car. There comes a point in any drive that long when all the video games and movies can no longer hold your attention. It's usually around this time in the trip that one of my boys will turn to me and ask, "Dad, would you tell us a story?"

They don't want to hear stories about Batman or Han Solo. Instead, they want me to tell them stories about *us*. They want to hear the stories about our family and about our adventures following God. I've tried to show my kids through the years that following Jesus in community is life's greatest adventure. And the stories we tell underscore that truth.

They love to hear the story about the time I was surrounded by neo-Nazis in Germany while preaching about Jesus—or the time we prayed for the rain to stop so our pontoon could reach its destination in the Philippines. God answered the prayer and stopped the rain. It was amazing.

I tell them about the time we got lost and almost died in a snowstorm in Iceland. We prayed, and God led us out of the storm. They love to hear the stories about how God was involved in each of their births. The Holy Spirit guided Mommy and me and built our family just the way he wanted it. I tell them and retell them. And every year, new stories are added to our family story. Every year, God does new miracles and reminds us again that *life with him was always supposed to be an adventure.*

The mission of Jesus was always intended to be a story of adventures, a story of *us*—how together we faced demons, overcame trials, endured hardships, and led people into eternity.

Is your life marked by God-inspired stories? Inspired by G. K. Chesterton, author N. D. Wilson wrote:

> We must tell stories the way God does, stories in which a sister must float her little brother on a river with nothing but a basket between him and the crocodiles. Stories in which a king is a coward, and a shepherd boy steps forward to face the giant.... Stories with dens of lions and fiery furnaces and lone prophets laughing at kings and priests and demons. Stories with heads on platters. Stories with courage and crosses and redemption. Stories with resurrections.[64]

These stories were never supposed to stay in the pages of Scripture. Scripture was written to teach us a way of life, because God is still writing miracle stories through our lives today.

What story is your life telling? Is it the story of how you never missed an episode of your favorite TV show? Is it the story of how you went to work every day and never mentioned Jesus to a single person? That's not the story he created you to write.

Maybe you need to buy an Elmo suit and pass out some flyers on the green. Maybe you need to pull over and help someone on the side of the road. Maybe you need to buy all the chairs for the building project at the church or join the prayer team so that when Javier comes up to the front for prayer, you're there to lead him to Jesus. What are you waiting for?

Imagine for a moment what the community of Jesus could look like if we *all* participated in this adventure. God's intention has always been that 100 percent of his church gives 100 percent of themselves for the mission of Jesus on earth. You and your friends could go serve the poor in a third-world country, or you could serve food at the local soup kitchen on Wednesday nights. You could host a barbecue and invite the neighbors. You could tutor kids after school who come from a rough neighborhood. The opportunities are everywhere.

Your life really could be a great adventure. But you are not called to go on the adventure alone. You could do it all with *us*—as part of God's great mission to make all things new. Because you were not created to do mission alone. Through the adventure of living for God, the Holy Spirit knits the hearts of his people together. Nothing forges a bond between people like adventure, and so often our

Christian communities lack depth because the mission has lost its edge. Who is taking a great risk for God? And who is taking someone with them? Your life will come alive when you find a small group of friends and advance the mission of Jesus together. Imagine the possibilities.

A while ago, I had a conversation with a friend who asked me about my recent vacation. I told him that my wife and I got away for a few days, laid low, and read some books. "That sounds kind of boring," he said. "Don't you want some adventure?"

The question made me chuckle. I thought of the time I prayed until it stopped raining in the Philippines and the time I prayed with Javier and his entire family was transformed by God. I thought about the Elmo suit, and Matt in the lobby, and Dale around the campfire. I thought about the stories I tell my kids.

"Honestly," I said, "we just wanted to rest. My *life* feels like an adventure."

I meant it lightheartedly, but the words hung in the air. And I realized that something was starting to change in me. Life was beginning to feel more and more like a real adventure.

Does your life ever feel like an adventure? Are you experiencing the thrill of making an eternal impact for God? If not, you can. Quoting a letter from his mother, author H. Jackson Brown Jr. wrote, "Twenty years from now you will be more disappointed by the things you didn't do than by the ones you did. So throw off the bowlines. Sail away from the safe harbor."[65]

That's pretty good advice. Too many Christians live in the safe harbor. But you were created for a mission. You are called to partner with God in his plan to make all things new. *Mission drives adventure.*

— SACRED STEPS —

As you reflect on the content of this chapter, consider taking the following steps to grow:

1. Read the book of Acts and ask God to ignite the spark of adventure in your heart. Then write down your three best adventures with God. Where has he worked miracles in your life? Share one of your stories with a close friend to inspire their faith.

2. Find two to three friends and volunteer to serve a community that's different from your own. It might be at a homeless shelter or a youth camp. It might be with single moms. After you serve, write down how the experience changed your heart and changed your relationship with your friends.

3. Plan to go on a mission trip with other Christians to a third-world country in the next three years. Get outside your cultural box and get a taste of the adventure of God beyond the borders of your everyday routines.

9

SACRIFICE MATURES LOVE

"Bring me a higher love. Where's that
higher love I keep thinking of?"[66]

Steve Winwood

"It is impossible to love deeply without sacrifice."[67]

Elisabeth Elliot

"Community is the fruit of our capacity to make the
interests of others more important than our own.... The
question, therefore, is not 'How can we make community?'
but 'How can we develop and nurture giving hearts?'"[68]

Henri Nouwen

"No one has ever seen God; but if we love one another,
God lives in us and his love is made complete in us."

1 John 4:12 NIV

Mia Dolan has big dreams to become a famous actress. Seb Wilder is an aspiring jazz musician. Through a random series of events, the two bump into each other and fall in love. At first, they aren't sure that their two unique lives could ever fit into one story. But the love is real, so both make adjustments for the sake of the relationship.

Mia's acting career struggles. Seb joins a band and things take off. Life becomes full of record deals and tours, and soon, Mia finds herself falling behind. She puts all her energy into performing her own one-person play, with Seb's encouragement. Then Seb misses Mia's big performance because of a photo shoot with his band. She's devastated. The couple breaks up. Mia moves back home with her parents and stops taking Seb's calls.

Eventually Mia's dreams come true, and she becomes a famous actress. Seb reaches his dreams also and owns a successful jazz club. Five years pass, and Mia is now married and has a daughter. One night, she and her husband wander into a club in Hollywood. It's the club Seb owns, and the former lovers lock eyes from across the room. Seb plays their favorite song, and both imagine what life would have been like if they had made it work. They never speak a word to each other. They don't have to. Both Mia and Seb have reached their dreams. They found success. And they did it at the expense of their love.

The movie *La La Land* went on to win seven Golden Globe Awards and six Academy Awards. It was considered a raving success and has become a favorite of movie lovers across the globe. But what's the appeal behind this movie? What pricked the hearts of so many viewers? Is it just the cinematography, the music, or the chemistry between the actors?

Anyone who's seen the movie knows that there's more. *La La Land* tells the story of *love*, and we all find a piece of ourselves somewhere in the story. The movie masterfully explores the tension between the love of *me* and the love of *us*. Every marriage, friendship, and community will feel this tension, and we will all wrestle with its many implications.

Who comes first in your priorities? What does it really mean to see your dreams come true? Does love for someone else fit into your plan, or should love lead you to change the plan? What *is* love anyway?

If we're honest, most of us haven't really thought deeply about these questions, and we walk into our friendships, our marriages, and our churches hoping to figure things out along the way. It doesn't take long before *love* complicates our relationships.

He spent the whole day golfing. Doesn't he want to see me?

She's so needy and always takes the things I say the wrong way. What is she so afraid of?

They all went out, but no one invited me. I wish someone would call to see how I'm doing.

I feel like everyone is talking about me behind my back. Is this what a loving community is supposed to look like?

Remember in chapter 7 when we examined the story of Abraham and Sarah and the son they named *Laughter*? If we zoom out far enough, the story can be told like this: God gave them the promise of a miracle son, and they trusted him perfectly all the way. Isaac was born, and through this lineage, Abraham became the father of many nations and the ancestor of Jesus.

But like all stories of love, the story of Abraham and Sarah is far more complex than it might look at first glance. It serves as an accurate picture of the deficiencies that mark all our significant relationships.

Long before Isaac and the fulfillment of God's promise, the couple traveled to Egypt. Because of Sarah's great beauty, Abraham was afraid the Egyptians would kill him and steal her. So, he lied to Pharaoh and told him that Sarah was his sister rather than his wife. This decision caused a host of problems, and Abraham's actions sent a clear message to his wife: *If it comes down to protecting me versus protecting you—I'm going to look out for me.*

His actions serve as an example of a *selfish heart.* A selfish heart is one that attempts to love others but doesn't really *see* others. Being so caught up in your own thing, you expect everyone else to orbit their lives around you.

You might leave your wife with the kids all day to hang out with your friends and never think to ask her what she wants to do. When you're in a conversation with a coworker, you aren't really listening to them as much as you are waiting for them to stop talking so that you can speak. You have the habit of checking a text on your phone when someone else is in the middle of a sentence. You want to be loved by others, but for you, love is about getting what you need from someone else. Like Abraham, you're ultimately looking out for number one. If the people in your life experience you this way, then you probably suffer from a *selfish heart.*

Growing up, I loved the book *The Missing Piece* by Shel Silverstein. It tells the story of a circle—which has a small slice cut out of it—that goes in search of its missing piece. The incomplete circle searches the whole world for its missing piece. It tries big pieces, small pieces, square pieces, and round pieces, but nothing seems to fit just right.

Then one day, the incomplete circle finds its missing piece. The circle is overjoyed that it's finally complete, but then it realizes that with its missing piece filled, it can no longer talk or sing. After searching its whole life and now finding its missing piece, the circle stops rolling and decides to part ways with the missing piece.

It would rather be incomplete than lose its ability to sing—something that it loves so much. And so goes the story of the *selfish heart*: always looking for the missing piece but unwilling to pay the price that comes with deep relationship.

The tragedy of the selfish heart is that those who have it usually don't know it until it's too late. King David couldn't see his selfish heart until an innocent man named Uriah had been killed and a woman named Bathsheba had been taken advantage of. Samson couldn't see his selfish heart until he was lying in prison with his eyes gouged out. Jacob couldn't see his selfish heart until he had wrestled with God and had his hip dislocated.

The selfish heart masterfully hides and deceives, convincing you that everyone else is the real problem. But it's not the only deficiency we carry into relationships. While Abraham was protecting himself at the expense of his wife, Sarah was dealing with her own issues. God had spoken to her husband, and they had left their homeland to pursue God's promise. But why hadn't God spoken to *her*?

For years, Sarah had been unable to have children, and she carried the shame of her barrenness every day. She felt useless. She felt incompetent. And as the years rolled by and the frustration grew, Sarah began to blame God. She eventually told Abraham to sleep with her servant Hagar so that at least he could have a child. She explained her reasoning in Genesis 16. "Behold now, the LORD *has prevented* me from bearing children. Go in to my servant" (Genesis 16:2).

Notice who she blamed for her infertility. God was the one behind her problems. Sarah was convinced that for some reason he was punishing her. She represents the second great problem we face when loving others. If Abraham represents the *selfish heart*, then Sarah is a living example of the *barren heart*.

When you live from a *barren heart*, you feel like you are always giving and others are always taking. You care so deeply for your friends, but you can't understand why they don't love you the way you love them. You'll sacrifice anything for your spouse, but it feels like no one takes the time for you.

The *barren heart* is always feeling like it's being taken advantage of, and it's always insecure—uncertain about the love of others. Love needs to be proven again and again, but it's never enough because the love you experience always leaks out so that the *barren heart* is never full.

As you read the descriptions of the selfish heart and the barren heart, it's easy to see these issues in the people closest to you. You might be thinking *That's exactly how my husband is* or *My best friend always does that*. But what about you? What broken version of love do you bring into your closest relationships?

The truth is that we all carry some of the *selfish heart* and some of the *barren heart* within ourselves. We all look for our missing piece and then end up still choosing ourselves. We all tend to care more about opening our own jazz club than we do about the dreams of another. And at some point, we all feel like our special someone didn't show up to our big day—like no one really cares about us. We are selfish and we are barren, and this makes love very complicated.

Abraham and Sarah continued in their dysfunction for decades until one day they had an encounter with El Shaddai. In Genesis 17,

God revealed himself by this name for the first time in Scripture. The name carries a host of meanings and can be translated "the Most Powerful," "the Almighty," or "the God who is Sufficient."

In this encounter, God also changed their names from Abram to Abraham and from Sarai to Sarah. He changed their names to mark a new beginning in their lives. God wanted to teach them something that every heart desperately needs to learn: *true identity and complete love must flow out of a relationship with him—the one who is all-sufficient.* In other words, you must personally encounter God as your all-sufficient one. It's from this personal encounter with him that, like Abram and Sarai, you discover your new name and learn to love in a whole new way.

The Peculiar God

Why did God give himself the name El Shaddai? What is this story intended to teach us? For one thing, it teaches us that God is not who we expect him to be. God is fundamentally different from us, and this is a challenging concept to grasp. Without realizing it, we often expect God to be like *us*—self-consumed, demanding, and hungry for attention. Every ancient depiction of deity follows that narrative, but El Shaddai is different. He is *peculiar*. He is so complete within himself that no trace of selfishness exists.

Through the trials of their lives, Abraham and Sarah learned that God really did love them and that his love was fundamentally different from anything they'd ever seen or anyone they'd ever met. Eventually, their hearts become convinced of his love—so much so that they would even put their son on an altar.

But how is the love of God so different from natural human love? The entire Bible paints the picture. God reveals the peculiarity of his love through the stories of the Old Testament. Through them, we find shadows and glimpses of a peculiar God.

The people who knew God throughout the Old Testament provide for us a glimpse of his nature. We see something in Moses, who chose suffering over the comforts of Egypt. We see something in Ruth, who remained faithful to her mother-in-law, even though no one would blame her if she abandoned the older woman. We see something in Joseph, who forgave his brothers, though they betrayed him and left him for dead.

These stories, along with dozens of others, are windows into the heart of God and bread crumbs on the path, leading us to God's ultimate demonstration of love. What God whispers through the stories of the Old Testament, he shouts through the story of Jesus. In his life, death, and resurrection, true love was put on full display and God revealed his heart for humanity. Jesus is the better Moses who left the treasure of heaven and the position of privilege to identify with us. He is the better Ruth who did not return to his homeland but remained faithful at his own expense. He is the better Joseph who rose from the prison of death and chose to forgive his brothers even though we didn't deserve it.

> What God whispers through the
> stories of the Old Testament, he
> shouts through the story of Jesus.

Moses gave up his privilege, Ruth gave up her homeland, and Joseph gave up his offense. Jesus did all of this and more, giving up his life for us. He came to reveal the greater and higher love of God and to restore humanity through an encounter with God's all-sufficiency.

Jesus introduced *agape* love into the human story. *Agape* is the Greek word used in the New Testament to express the love of God. It's fundamentally different from human love and challenges the concepts of love that we naturally hold. Agape love is a love that gives for the benefit of others. It's a love without strings attached, that doesn't look for bargains or even fair trades.

Agape love tends to offend our natural sensibilities. Where human love often comes from a place of need, agape love comes from a place of deep inner fulfillment. Rather than making bargains, agape just makes itself second. The supply of agape can flow from only the heart of God, since God alone is a river that never runs dry. "Love bears all things, believes all things, hopes all things, endures all things. Love never ends" (1 Corinthians 13:7–8).

Is it possible to live with a love like that? What would a community marked by God's agape love look like?

Maybe you've heard of the duck-billed platypus. When scientists first discovered this creature in the late 1700s, they were convinced it was just a mammal. It had fur like a mammal and a tail that resembled a beaver's. But the platypus laid eggs like a bird and had a stinger like a scorpion. It was a scientific anomaly, and it didn't fit into any known category or species.

The agape love of God is a lot like a platypus. We try to understand it through our categories, and we are left without an answer. It doesn't fit into any box we have, and so we must learn to receive it for what it is. Like a platypus, God's love for us just *shouldn't be*—and yet it is—present, available, and overflowing.

Take a moment to allow the truth of his peculiar love to sink a little deeper. First, God's love is an *undeserved* love. "You see, at just the right time, when we were still powerless, Christ died for the ungodly. Very rarely will anyone die for a righteous person, though for a good person someone might possibly dare to die. But God demonstrates his own love for us in this: *While we were still sinners, Christ died for us*" (Romans 5:6–8 NIV). The love of God comes independently of our good deeds. He didn't die for the good people. He died for all people. And his love can be deeply received only when we embrace the truth that it is undeserved.

Second, the love of God is a *costly* love. "Greater love has no one than this: to lay down one's life for one's friends" (John 15:13 NIV). To make this love available to us cost Jesus his life. How much is the life of the incarnate God worth? The value of his life is beyond calculation, yet he willingly paid the price.

Third, God's love is a *voluntary* love. It isn't forced or obligated. It flows freely from his own choice. "No one can take my life from me. I sacrifice it voluntarily. For I have the authority to lay it down when I want to and also to take it up again" (John 10:18 NLT). Jesus made the choice. No one forced him to do it. Not even his Father made him. He chose. And he wanted to.

Fourth, it is a *beneficial* love. It provides the benefit of eternal life for all who believe. "For God *so loved* the world that he gave his one and only Son, that whoever believes in him shall not perish but *have eternal life*" (John 3:16 NIV). This is the greatest benefit imaginable, since the essence of eternal life is to know God (John 17:3).

The love of God is *undeserved, costly, voluntary*, and *beneficial*. It is God's greatest platypus, unable to fit into any category or box that we try to build. When we trust in the agape love of God, agape itself changes us. We discover the radical sufficiency of God's love. As God did with Abraham and Sarah, the truth of God's love *renames* us. No longer do we need to cling to a selfish heart. The selflessness of Jesus breaks the spell of our own selfishness.

No longer do we need to live with a barren heart. God has loved us more perfectly than we ever could have imagined. Paul explained this transformation when he wrote, "Christ's love *controls* us. Since we believe that Christ died for all, we also believe that we have all died to our old life. He died for everyone so that those who receive his new life will no longer live for themselves. Instead, they will live for Christ, who died and was raised for them" (2 Corinthians 5:14–15 NLT).

The Greek word translated "controls" literally means "holds together." Like many fractured pieces scattered across a room, Jesus collects the fragments of your heart and rebuilds it. Now you are held together by his love.

And it was never intended to remain as a personal, individual experience. As this truth is believed and received by individuals, the agape love of God forms a new sacred community.

Of all the characteristics of biblical community that we have considered, agape love stands at the very center. "By this everyone will know that you are my disciples, *if you love* one another" (John 13:35 NIV). It was always God's intention that his act of love *for* us would create a new power to love *in* us, and this new power to love *in us* would be the defining characteristic *among* us. Christians have been redefined by the love of God, leading to a community that serves, gives, considers, honors, prefers, and sacrifices like no other community on earth. Agape love is the secret of Christian community.

Throughout the history of the church, followers of Jesus have experienced the power of God's love for them and then found the power to express that love back to the world. Richard Wurmbrand, the Romanian pastor who spent over a decade in prison for his faith at the hands of Communist leaders, wrote about this love:

> I have seen Christians in Communist prisons with fifty pounds of chains on their feet, tortured with red-hot iron pokers, in whose throats spoonfuls of salt had been forced, being kept afterward without water, starving, whipped, suffering from cold—and praying with fervor for the Communists. This is humanly inexplicable! It is the love of Christ, which was poured out in our hearts.[69]

When I consider Wurmbrand's words, my heart burns to learn and practice a love like that. It was always God's intention for this peculiar love to be the defining mark of his people. When Jesus explained his plan in the Sermon on the Mount, he said, "If you greet only your brothers, *what more* are you doing than others?" (Matthew 5:47).

Christian community must be marked by a *what more*. This means that there is something uncommon—something remarkable or extraordinary—about the people of God. Every person loves someone or something to a degree. But Christians carry God's *what more*. We don't need to be known in the world for our extraordinary talent or our amazing programs. But we are called to be known for our uncommon, remarkable love.

As you reflect on your experience with church and Christian community, do you see this type of love? Are we, in fact, marked by agape?

Learning to Love

When most followers of Jesus measure the agape love in our lives, we find that it's lacking both in ourselves and in our relationships. Yet Jesus does not simply encourage us to love. He commands us to love. "A new command I give you: Love one another. As I have loved you, so you *must* love one another" (John 13:34 NIV). This scripture can be a bit puzzling at first. How can Jesus command me to love? How can I control what I feel? Sometimes love is there, and sometimes it's not—what does he expect me to do?

Our frustration exposes our own misunderstanding of the essence of love. We often think of love primarily as an emotion—a deep sense of care or compassion for someone or something. But according to Scripture, love is far more (and sometimes a bit less) than an emotion. Love is an *action*. Love is a choice. Biblical scholar R. C. Sproul wrote, "In the New Testament, love is more of a verb than a noun. It has more to do with acting than with feeling. The call to love is not so much a call to a certain state of feeling as it is to a quality of action."[70]

Christians must learn to *act* in love before we *feel* in love. C. S. Lewis added, "Do not waste time bothering whether you 'love' your neighbor; act as if you did."[71] Jesus has commanded us to love one another, and it is within our control to obey his command. So, you and I must choose to love, again and again, when we feel it and when we feel nothing. But what does choosing to love really look like?

Of course, we've already seen the answer. We've seen agape love in Moses when he left the comforts of Egypt. We've seen it in Ruth when she said goodbye to her homeland. We've seen it in Joseph when he let go of his offense toward his brothers. Finally, we've seen it in all its perfection in Jesus—when he hung on the cross. Choosing to love looks like *sacrifice*.

In the movie *La La Land*, it was sacrifice that was missing between Mia and Seb. They had a strong attraction for each other and great chemistry, but their love didn't last because neither one was willing to sacrifice. Love without sacrifice is like a gift-wrapped box with nothing inside. It looks like the real thing, but it's empty. Amy Carmichael wrote, "You can always give without loving, but you can never love without giving."[72] Written into the DNA of agape love is the requirement of sacrifice. It's unavoidable. And until you choose sacrifice, God's love can't be expressed through you.

But sacrifice doesn't just *express* God's love through you. It also *expands* God's love in you. Every time you choose to sacrifice, your capacity to contain the love of God gets bigger. The apostle John wrote, "No one has ever seen God; if we love one another, God abides in us and his love is *perfected* in us" (1 John 4:12). The Greek word behind "perfected" means "to be made complete" or "to fully carry through." God develops his love in you as you act in love toward others. If you don't act, agape doesn't grow. This is the sixth principle of biblical community: *sacrifice matures love*.

We see a beautiful picture of sacrificial love in the story of Mary, who broke her alabaster jar of pure nard and washed the feet of Jesus before the crucifixion (Mark 14:3–9; John 12:1–8). Normally, an expensive perfume like this was dabbed on in small quantities, and the contents of the jar might last a lifetime. But Mary used the entire jar in a moment. The disciples of Jesus were shocked since the perfume was worth about a year's wage. It seemed like a waste to sacrifice all the perfume at one time.

> Love without sacrifice is like a gift-wrapped box with nothing inside.

But Jesus wanted to teach us that *unreasonableness* is a distinguishing mark of his love. Loving with agape will often seem unwise or even wasteful. It will look like you're going too far and you're giving too much. Your sacrifice might seem irresponsible. But isn't the cross itself unreasonable? Didn't God give too much and go too far? And why are we so averse to looking unreasonable? When was the last time you were accused of going too far for an act of love? This might be at the heart of what so many Christian communities are missing.

Notice how Jesus defended Mary's actions. He said that she had done "what she *could*" (Mark 14:8). He didn't say that she had done what she *should*. Obligation or duty was not her motivation. Agape love chooses to sacrifice, and the sacrifice should align with what God has entrusted to you. Mary had perfume, and she did what she could with what she had. In the same way, God has put something unique in your hand. He's given you something—maybe a talent or a treasure. What will you do with what you've been given? Will you hold on to the gift and keep it for yourself, or will you spend it on Jesus and be left with nothing?

But Mary wasn't left with nothing. The story ends with some of the most encouraging words in all the Bible: "And truly, I say to you, wherever the gospel is proclaimed in the whole world, what she has done will be told in memory of her" (Mark 14:9). No one would have ever cared about that perfume if she hadn't emptied the bottle on the feet of Jesus. But her life was marked with eternal significance because she practiced an unreasonable love. What about us? What mark are we leaving? What memory will be retold of us?

For far too long, Christians have talked about love, prayed about love, read scriptures about love, and complained about the lack of love that we see in the church. But love grows only by doing. *Sacrifice matures love*, and biblical community grows as you decide to stretch.

Stretching Further

Do you have a plan to stretch your love? What sacrifice are you making right now so that your love can mature? Most of us don't have very thoughtful answers to these questions. I've recognized through the years that I am an expert at avoiding sacrifice. I come up with excuses that sound godly, but at the root they're selfish.

I can't give that much money to the church. I need to be more responsible and save for my kids' college. God wouldn't want our family to be unprepared for the future ...

I can't volunteer as a tutor for those kids in the projects on Tuesday afternoon. I need to work and be a good steward at my job. God wouldn't want me falling behind ...

There's something in all of us that naturally seeks to insulate ourselves from discomfort. We sense the inconvenience of sacrificing, and our "excuse generator" starts cranking out options. What we often don't realize is that our excuses actually rob us of the hidden joy of love. This is why we must learn to see beyond the discomfort and catch a glimpse of the heart of God. On the other side of sacrifice there is a joy far greater than the loss.

Years ago, when Chrisy and I first got married, we felt God asking us to invite a young guy named Sam to come and stay with us. Truthfully, I didn't really want Sam living at our house. He was messy, and we were newlyweds. But every time we prayed, we felt that God was saying *Do it*, so we finally invited Sam to stay, and he ended up being the first of many people to live with us through the years.

Each time we said yes to God and opened our home, it came with a cost. But what we didn't realize was that through every yes, God was stretching our love and preparing our hearts for a far greater joy. Time went by, and our experiments with intentional community continued. We had our first child, and then our second. Soon, our little family was a community unto itself.

We bought a second house, and both our homes overflowed with people. More friends joined us, and after a couple of years, our church had dozens of people living in close proximity and doing life together. Then we planted new churches, and a number of our neighbors moved away to start new locations. It seemed that the seasons were changing, and Chrisy and I both felt that God was preparing us for something new.

By this time, we had three sons and we had lived in some form of sacrificial, intentional community for over fifteen years. Hadn't we done enough? Wasn't it time to buy a house in the suburbs and tell everyone else to leave us alone?

It was at this point that God whispered to our hearts his next step for our family. It came to Chrisy in prayer. It was confirmed for me through James 1:27: "True devotion, the kind that is pure and faultless before God the Father, is this: *to care for orphans* and widows in their difficulties" (James 1:27 CEB). We both felt the same nudge from God: he was calling us to adopt a child who didn't have a home.

With three kids and a busy life already, it took some inner wrestling for me to say yes. I wanted to obey God, but there was still something inside of me that wanted *my* life. Have you ever felt that tension? Over time, however, God had been teaching me the secret of sacrifice: *that on the other side of sacrifice he hides his joy.* We eventually decided to pursue adoption.

At first, we looked at adoption agencies. We felt like these allowed for a little more predictability in the process. The transaction seemed clean. We would get paired with a child, sign the papers, pay the fees, and that would be it. But every time we prayed, we felt that this wasn't the path God had for us. Hundreds of kids in Connecticut, where we live, were stuck in the foster care system without a family. No one wanted these kids, and God had called us to give our lives for intentional community in this place. If these children lived in our city and they had no options, then shouldn't the people of God step up?

Kids in the foster care system come from complicated situations. They have been removed from their homes due to abuse or neglect. In many cases, the birth parents are still very much involved. Nothing is clean. Nothing goes as planned. With a wife and three kids, I was concerned that we might be biting off a little more than we could chew.

I remember thinking: *Maybe we could just adopt a child through an agency ... Foster care just seems unreasonable. Other people might be called to do that, but our life is so full already. It just feels unwise to get involved in this ...*

I thought of Mary and her alabaster jar. That was unreasonable. I thought of Joseph forgiving his brothers and Ruth staying with Naomi. I thought of Jesus. Everything about God's love is inconvenient and unreasonable. Why was I trying to edit the process?

We wrestled with our next step for months until God clearly spoke to Chrisy one day in prayer: *"I've given you the grace to adopt through the state."* She felt this impression so strongly, and the more I prayed about it, the more I felt God confirm the decision in my heart. We enrolled in classes to become foster parents.

At the same time that we finished our licensing as foster parents, we also sold our house on Earl Street. Community for us was changing. The closing of our new house was delayed, which meant that Connecticut would not license our family without a permanent address. So, we waited another nine months until we moved into our new house, and we were finally approved.

Just days after getting licensed, we received a phone call. There was a three-day-old baby girl who needed a home. Her mom had used multiple drugs throughout the pregnancy, and the effects on this little girl were unknown. They didn't know who the dad was. Shortly after receiving the call, Chrisy and I were at the hospital. As soon as we met this little girl, we sensed that we were holding the next member of our family.

Thea Rose came home with us a couple of days later. We got to know her birth mom and eventually met her birth dad after a DNA test. For the first six months, her little body was detoxing from the drugs. We would hold her for hours every night while she cried, and her body shook in our arms. Sometimes we were afraid, sometimes heartbroken, and sometimes we were just plain exhausted. I can clearly remember lying in bed late Saturday night with a tiny baby girl shaking on my chest as I looked at the clock.

I've got to get up in two hours and go preach at three church services, I thought. *I haven't slept for more than an hour ...* Then the thoughts of doubt would come flooding back. *God, I can't do this. It's unreasonable ...*

Over the course of the first six months, God continued to stretch us. He uncovered selfishness in me that I didn't know was there. He exposed my fears and tested the limits of my faith. With each passing day, every little sacrifice chipped away at my heart and reshaped it into something different. I wanted this, but still my flesh was squirming.

God was making new space to love that our family didn't have before. After a few months, I noticed how we were all changing for the better because of Thea Rose. I saw it in my boys. I saw it in my wife. This little girl was a Kendrick. And we knew that she was *home.*

And then we got the phone call. A relative of Thea's had come forward and requested custody of the child. We were told that Thea would be leaving our home as soon as the transition was complete. The news came like a hurricane. Of course, we wanted what was best for this little girl, but this was unexpected. It was everything we'd feared, and we were not in control.

We met the family member who had come forward, and she was *great.* She was loving, caring, thoughtful, and kind. The state made the final decision to move Thea into her care, and then it was only a matter of formalities.

Our hearts were caught in a tailspin of emotions, and saying goodbye felt like open-heart surgery. We sat our boys down and told them the news, and together we *wept*. I will never forget the feeling of holding my sons as the five of us sobbed and mourned our baby's departure.

Along with the pain of goodbye, each time Chrisy and I prayed, we kept sensing the Holy Spirit say that the story was not over. We didn't even want to say it out loud, but we both felt that God would make a way for Thea to stay with us. Was that just wishful thinking? Were we in denial? We weren't sure how to pray or what to do, but one thing became clear: through this process, God was stretching our love.

The transition lasted months, and we did numerous visits. Every day our hearts walked through a kaleidoscope of feelings. From hurt, to hope, to anger, to sadness—we weren't sure what we should feel. We had chosen this, and we knew when we signed up that it would be difficult. With each passing visit, the transition became more permanent. We reminded ourselves that in the end, none of this was about *us*. It was always about *love*, and God had never said that love would be easy.

On the second-to-last visit before Thea would officially leave our home, we sat down to discuss plans with her relative. By this time, we had built a good relationship with a few members of her birth family. We sat in our living room. Our little girl was still napping. And then with one conversation, *everything changed*.

The family member who had asked for custody had prayerfully decided to withdraw the request. She wanted Thea to stay with us. And this meant that we could move forward to adoption.

We were stunned. We held hands, wept together, and prayed. It was one of the most sacred moments of my life. Our love had been stretched, and when things were completely beyond our control, God had moved. He fulfilled the word he'd whispered to Chrisy all those months before: "I've given you the grace to *adopt* through the state."

The adoption was finalized a few months later, and we added a new member to the Kendrick family. We chose Thea Rose. And her family chose us. Above all, God chose to use this circumstance to stretch our love, and we learned once again that on the other side of sacrifice, there is joy. When we finally received the certificate of adoption, one sentence in the adoption decree especially caught my attention:

"He or she will be treated as if he or she were the biological child of the adopting parent for all purposes."

Tears still come to my eyes when I read that sentence. It embodies the heart of the gospel. Her name, *Thea*, means "God's gift," and that is exactly who she is to us. She's already taught us so much, and the joy she brings to our family is beyond anything we could have imagined.

Thea is one more example of the process of agape in our lives. *Sacrifice matures love.* What if we had avoided the pain? What if we had seen the challenges of foster care and just walked away? What if we hadn't listened to that inner whisper of the Holy Spirit?

We would have missed one of life's greatest joys. We would have missed our daughter. I have made countless mistakes in life, but I am so grateful for God's sustaining grace in this circumstance. In our own strength, we certainly would have chosen the comfortable road. But God doesn't leave us in our own strength.

Through sacrifice, God expands our love and changes the essence of sacrifice itself. We come to realize that what we thought was *sacrificial* turns out to be *beneficial*. What we gain from love is far greater than what we give through sacrifice. This is the paradox of love.

Mother Teresa said it best: "I have found the paradox, that if you love until it hurts, there can be no more hurt, only more love."[73] Every time love gives, love grows, because a love that gives touches the heart of God. He is a well that never runs dry. But love grows only when we act before we feel.

Imagine for a moment living in a community of people who believed and applied this truth. What impact could we make? What type of people could we become? Every day, I fight feelings of selfishness and barrenness that exist within me. I find myself reverting back to *La La Land* love—the kind that puts personal ambition ahead of willful sacrifice. I forget what I've learned, and I have to remind myself again.

> What we gain from love is far greater than what we give through sacrifice. This is the paradox of love.

But I have noticed something changing: little by little, my love is growing. I'm less afraid of the cost and more convinced of the joy. And I want to go further. *Sacrifice matures love.*

— SACRED STEPS —

As you reflect on the content of this chapter, consider taking the following steps to grow:

1. Review the section on *selfish* love and *barren* love. Write down in a journal where you see these two characteristics in your life. Review the last three to six months and identify moments where *selfish* love and *barren* love have been at work in you.

2. Consider giving away something sacred to you—a prized possession, an expensive trinket, or a sum of money. Don't do this out of obligation or duty. Do it to attach your heart to God's heart and grow in love. Pray for guidance about what you should give and who you should give it to. Then follow through.

3. Begin to pray weekly about one major sacrifice that God would have you make over the next three to five years. Consider something that would significantly alter your life. Should you pursue foster care or adoption? Should you welcome an elderly parent into your home? Should you make a life-altering financial sacrifice? Once you have identified the sacrifice, begin planning the road map, then take the next step forward.

10

BOUNDARIES SUSTAIN GROWTH

"Boundaries define us. They define *what is me* and *what is not me*. A boundary shows me where I end and someone else begins, leading me to a sense of ownership. Knowing what I am to own and take responsibility for gives me freedom."[74]

Henry Cloud

"The beginning of this love is the will to let those we love be perfectly themselves, the resolution not to twist them to fit our own image. If in loving them we do not love what they are, but only their potential likeness to ourselves, then we do not love them: we only love the reflection of ourselves we find in them."[75]

Thomas Merton

"I go to put my arm around you, and you give me a look like I'm way out of bounds."[76]

Bruce Springsteen

"For each will have to bear his own load."

Galatians 6:5

It was fourth down and we still had a long way to go. My son Noah was running a deep route, hoping for a bomb that would score him a touchdown. I threw the ball, and Noah made a diving catch in the sand, only to have my oldest son, Gabe, quickly wrap him up and push him to the ground. "You're out of bounds!" Gabe yelled.

"No, my feet were in. That was a good catch."

Beach football with the Kendrick family is not always cut and dried. The argument continued until it was finally decided by a game of rock-paper-scissors. The play was just too close to call. It's difficult to run in the sand, and since we usually only have four players, some of the rules need to be adjusted. But the most frustrating thing about beach football isn't the burning sand or the foggy rules. It's the *boundary lines*.

No matter how hard you try, the field of play is never quite right. One end zone turns out to be bigger than the other, and the out-of-bounds line that we create by dragging a sandal through the sand squiggles back and forth. Sometimes a game will be ruined by a technicality, like whether or not Noah's feet were in bounds on the final catch. My boys are competitive, and there are times when the arguments go on for days. Was he in? Noah certainly thinks so, but Gabe is convinced that his right foot was out. The truth is that the boundaries were so blurry that a clear call is impossible.

Life is full of boundaries. We have to set boundaries on our time, boundaries on our schedule, and boundaries on our relationships. But what do we do when the boundaries of life are unclear? Most of the time, we argue. We tend to see the information in a way that most benefits us and then push that point of view as far as we can.

The world is full of unclear boundaries, and it's eroding trust and ruining relationships every day. All around us, people are suffering from *boundary dysfunction*. We give too little and ruin a relationship, or we give too much and it nearly kills us. Have you ever examined the boundaries in your life?

Some people can't seem to *turn off*. We constantly check our phones and our email. We don't want to miss that big business deal, and we don't want to miss out on what's happening in the world. The constant flood of social media and news stories keeps us *on*, and we often feel like we have to keep checking. What if something happens or someone needs to get ahold of us?

This inability to turn off is like playing a football game with no boundary lines. The field is the whole world—run wherever you want. Anyone can call or email or message you at any moment, and you have to respond. Your time is not your own. But if we remove all the boundaries, doesn't it eventually destroy the game?

Some people can't say yes when opportunities arise. We're afraid of commitment and functionally overbooked, so we say only maybe and no. Your church asks for volunteers, but you're too busy. A friend invites you to a small group, but you can't make it. Sometimes we are so driven by our own agenda that we have no room even to be led by God. Our Alcatraz-like boundaries are keeping us from real community, and no matter who invites us to what, we just can't make it fit.

There are those who do a good job of turning off and saying yes. But they can't seem to say no. Someone needs a ride to church, and right away you say yes. Someone needs you to cover their shift at work, and without looking at your other commitments, you say yes. Someone invites you over for dinner—and you're out every other night this week—but you still say yes. It seems that everyone else is setting the agenda for your life. Then a friend asks if you can help them remodel their bathroom. You find yourself squeezing it in and saying yes. Your life is buckling under the pressure of your constant yeses, and you're losing any sense of purpose or direction. Is this the way God intended us to live?

A while ago, I was sitting at my desk at home. Looking out the window, I noticed a piece of trash stuck in one of my bushes. I couldn't tell what it was, but it was ugly. *I gotta get that trash out of that bush*, I thought. But then I got busy with something else and did nothing. The next day, I noticed it again. I said the same thing to myself and still did nothing. Weeks went by and the pattern continued. Finally, I could take it no longer. One day, I simply stopped what I was doing, walked into my backyard, and pulled the piece of trash out of the bush.

It was a balloon with an image of a monkey on it. It had probably slipped out of the hands of some kid miles away and the wind had carried it into my yard. I stood there staring at this monkey balloon, thinking about the weeks it had remained in my yard while I had complained about it but done nothing. Someone else's trash had become my problem and I had just left it, unwilling to walk outside, deal with it, and throw it away.

Our lives are a lot like that yard. We need to tend it, care for it, and be intentional about what we let in. For those of us who can't turn off, we don't even know there's a monkey balloon stuck in the bush. We're too preoccupied to be engaged with the world around us, so things pile up, and pretty soon it's obvious that our house is not in order.

For those of us who can't say yes, our blinds are down and our windows are closed. Opportunities and problems may come, but we see only the interior walls. We miss the moments that God would have us engage.

For those of us who can't say no, someone else's monkey balloon has floated into our space, and we let it get stuck in the bushes of our lives. We might complain, but we're unwilling to defend our boundaries. Pretty soon, the yard looks like a dump—full of other people's problems that have somehow floated in.

Why do so many Christians seem to struggle with boundaries? Part of the reason is we follow a Savior who taught us to "go the extra mile" and "give your enemy the shirt off your back," which leads many to believe that we can't say no. We try saying yes to everything for a while, and eventually we get jaded and calloused. Soon, we've shut the blinds and make no our default answer to every opportunity.

What's gone wrong? How do we know what's in bounds and what's out of bounds?

Learning Boundaries

When Chrisy and I first started the church, we had such a deep passion for biblical community that we felt the need to be at the center of all the activity. We started a small group at our house, and it quickly overflowed with people, so we started a second group on another night. I met with guys one on one for spiritual growth nearly every day of the week. When the phone rang, we answered. When someone had a need, we stopped what we were doing and went to help.

Our hearts were pure, but our plan was terrible. It didn't take long before my wife and kids felt neglected, and my soul felt empty.

This couldn't be the way God intended the family of God to work. What were we missing?

In his letter to the Galatians, Paul gave some important advice about boundaries.

> Bear one another's burdens, and so fulfill the law of Christ. For if anyone thinks he is something, when he is nothing, he deceives himself. But let each one test his own work, and then his reason to boast will be in himself alone and not in his neighbor. For each will have to bear his own load. (Galatians 6:2–5)

At first, this passage seems like a contradiction. He tells us to bear one another's burdens, then two verses later he tells us to carry our own load. Which one is it? Paul is sharing an incredible insight around biblical boundaries, because it's *both*.

The word translated "burdens" in the text means "a trouble, a weight"—something too heavy for you to carry. Imagine a boulder that weighs so much that no matter how hard you push, it isn't moving. Every person will face a few boulders. Maybe your sister was just diagnosed with cancer. Maybe your wife just left you for another man. Maybe you recently found out that your son has a learning disability that will define his life. Some things are just too heavy to carry on your own. Paul calls these things *burdens*.

If you see your brother getting crushed by a burden and you avoid him, then you've broken the law of Christ to love your neighbor as yourself. Burdens require the strength of community to endure, and *everyone* will need that strength at some point.

This is difficult for some of us, because while we like the idea of helping another person carry a burden, we are uncomfortable letting others help us carry ours. "I'm fine," you say every time people ask you how you're doing. But you're not fine—you're getting crushed, and you can't grow until you learn to ask others for help. God made life in such a way that everyone needs help sometimes, and he created the people of God so that we can learn to let others help us.

> Burdens require the strength of community to endure, and *everyone* will need that strength at some point.

But not every problem in life is a burden, and not everything requires the help of someone else. That's why Paul said two verses later, "For each will have to bear his *own load*" (Galatians 6:5). He used the word *load* to distinguish it from the burdens he just described. This word *load* means "cargo." It was a word used with ships that carried cargo from one destination to another. The "load" was the amount of cargo a particular ship was designed to carry. In other words, God made you to carry the load of your life, and *only you can carry your cargo.*

My friend Lance Witt likes to say, "You are ridiculously responsible for your own life." You're responsible for your behavior, your attitude, your choices, and your feelings. You must take responsibility for your money and your relationships. No one can—and no one should—carry these things for you. Of course, there are exceptions in life. Sometimes an illness or a tragedy can change things, but in those cases someone's cargo has become a real burden and help is appropriate.

Years ago, I talked to a married couple on the verge of divorce and the husband said, "I'm ready to give up. I'm just not happy in the relationship anymore." Consider the implications behind those words. When did it become the responsibility of the relationship to make you happy? Can any relationship thrive under that pressure?

The uncomfortable truth is that it's not your spouse's job to make you happy. No one else can be ultimately responsible for your happiness other than you. That's your cargo, and if you ask someone else to carry it, the relationship won't work. When you don't understand the difference between your burden and your cargo, you end up tumbling into at least one of these four pitfalls.

THE FOUR PITFALLS OF HEALTHY BOUNDARIES

1. SELFISHNESS:	2. PRIDE:
I WON'T HELP WITH MY BROTHER'S BURDEN	I WON'T SHARE MY BURDEN WITH OTHERS
3. CODEPENDENCE:	4. ENABLING:
I DON'T TAKE RESPONSIBILITY FOR MY CARGO	I CARRY OTHER PEOPLE'S CARGO

Pitfall 1 is *selfishness*. This person is unwilling to suffer the pain of helping someone else carry a burden. It feels too costly. What they don't realize is that they will never be able to build meaningful relationships until they are willing to enter into the pain of another.

Remember, sacrifice matures love.

Pitfall 2 is *pride*. This person is quick to help a friend, but they never let anyone help them carry *their* burdens. They might look strong on the outside, but they're a mess on the inside.

God made you to need others, and until you let other people in, pride will destroy your closest relationships.

Pitfall 3 is *codependence*. This person won't take responsibility for their own cargo. They expect someone else to do for them what they refuse to do for themselves. They are always in need, and they always seem to have a new emergency.

This mindset of "the victim" fools you into thinking that everyone is against you, when in fact you are your own biggest enemy. Nothing changes until you pick up your cargo and carry it for yourself.

Pitfall 4 is *enabling*. This person can't say no to people around them, not realizing that their acts of kindness are often perpetuating the problem. They are carrying other people's cargo, and it's exhausting for them and enabling for others.

Dr. Henry Cloud provided great insight into this problem:

> When we begin to set boundaries with people we love, a really hard thing happens: they hurt. They may feel a hole where you used to plug up their aloneness, their disorganization, or their financial irresponsibility. Whatever it is, they will feel a loss.

> If you love them, this will be difficult for you
> to watch. But, when you are dealing with someone
> who is hurting, remember that your boundaries
> are both necessary for you and helpful for them.
> If you have been enabling them to be irrespon-
> sible, your limit setting may nudge them toward
> responsibility.[77]

Which pitfall do you most often stumble into? And how do you know when someone else's problem is a burden you should help carry or is cargo that they need to carry themselves? How do you know when to invite others into one of your problems or take responsibility to carry it? These distinctions can often be difficult to discern, but sandwiched between Paul's commands about burdens and cargo is a helpful insight: "For if anyone thinks he is something, when he is nothing, he deceives himself" (Galatians 6:3).

Doesn't that feel a little harsh? What does Paul mean? He's teaching us that the primary thing that makes boundaries blurry in relationships is when you *think you are something*. A self-centered perspective is the natural condition of sinful humanity. But when your sense of self is built on comparison and achievement, you will either wallow in your failures or you will strut in your accom-plishments. Either way, this need to *think you're something* leads to self-deception.

The gospel cripples our strut when it proclaims that "*all* have sinned" (Romans 3:23) and that our righteous deeds are like filthy rags to God (Isaiah 64:6). It requires that you look at your own bro-kenness before you judge your brother (Matthew 7:5), and the result is *humility*. Humility in your heart is like a new pair of glasses. It enables you to see your need for God and your need for others, and it prevents you from hiding behind excuses, because God holds you responsible for your sin.

But the gospel uncovers your *sinfulness* and affirms your *beloved-ness* at the same time, since the same God who exposes your sin washes it away with the blood of his Son. You are more sinful than you thought and at the same time more loved than you deserve. The cross, then, sets you free from shame and comparisons, teaching your heart humility while offering you an unshakable confidence.

Now, in the light of grace, you can discover who God made you to be. "But let each one test his own work, and then his reason to boast will be in himself alone and not in his neighbor" (Galatians 6:4). Humility sets your heart free to realize that *I am not the same as you*. We have different gifts and abilities. We have different callings, and God does not compare us. You can build an identity based on the grace of God rather than on comparison to others. The gospel teaches us humility and identity, and this is what provides clarity in our relationships.

humility + identity = clarity

As the gospel sinks into your heart and informs the way you see yourself, it frees you to set healthy boundaries. You can turn off your phone and not be afraid that you're missing out. You can say yes or you can say no, depending on the situation. You can love others deeply and sacrifice much but still have more to give. You can invite others into your struggles and take responsibility for your life at the same time. You can ask for help, and you can weep with the one who is hurting.

This is the seventh principle of biblical community, and it's here that we develop the structures that allow for healthy relationships over the long haul. *Boundaries sustain growth.*

> Humility in your heart is like a new pair of glasses. It enables you to see your need for God and your need for others.

When Christians practice the first six principles of biblical community outlined in this book, things will begin to grow. Proximity provides opportunity, vulnerability creates connection, discipleship sets direction, fun amplifies grace, mission drives adventure, and sacrifice matures love. But these principles can't thrive without God-inspired boundaries.

What would a community look like that maintained healthy boundaries?

It would require that we ask an appropriate amount from the various degrees of relationships. Not all relationships operate on the same level, and though we owe all people love, we can't give all people the same degree of access or commitment.

Relationships operate at various depths. Some will stay at a surface level. Others will go deeper. The following graphic illustrates six different levels of relationship.

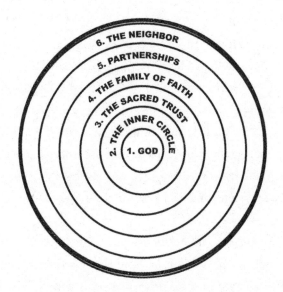

As we reflect on these various levels of relationship, it's important to note that there is a sense of fluidity between them. Life is not mechanical. No one can or should perfectly categorize every person in their lives into one of these levels. However, understanding the various levels of relationship can help us create clear expectations with the different people in our lives.

The deepest relationship in the life of a believer must be a personal relationship with **God**. This is circle number one. No one else can fill this role. We must pursue God for ourselves and get to know him in a personal and secret way. Of course, community teaches us aspects of God that we cannot learn otherwise, but community can never take the place of a one-on-one relationship with him.

Knowing God personally should never become an excuse to avoid deep community. You need *both* a secret relationship with God and close relationships with other believers. The nature of this "me and

God" relationship is *eternal*. You belong to him forever. The defining characteristic of this relationship is that it serves as your *source*. God is your ultimate source of love, value, purpose, and identity.

When this is true, it creates a healthy core for all other relationships in life. When this is not true, you will look for others to answer the questions that only God can answer. *Am I valuable? Do I have purpose?* Soon, relationships in your life will crumble under the weight of those questions, but the relationships aren't the problem. The problem is that you asked a person to be for you what only God can be.

The second level of relationship is **The Inner Circle**. These are the closest people in your life, and this level of relationship can usually fit only one to three other people. If you are married, this includes your spouse, and your spouse must hold priority over anyone else. You might also have a very close friend, a sister, or a parent at this level. The nature of this relationship is *covenantal*. The defining characteristic is that it is a lifelong commitment. These people are very special and very rare, and this level takes a lifetime to build.

You can be what you need to be for the people in your Inner Circle only when you look to God to be what he must be for you. If God is not at the center of your life, you will naturally try to expand this circle beyond one to three people and look to them to be your source. To do this will put an unhealthy strain on your Inner Circle and will leave you constantly disappointed.

The third level of relationship is **The Sacred Trust**. The nature of these relationships is *personal*, and the defining characteristic is *mutual sacrifice*. This might include your nuclear family, close friendships, or people in your community group. It might also include key mentors in your life.

This layer of relationship differs from your Inner Circle in that people will transition in or out of your Sacred Trust more frequently. Where the intention of the Inner Circle is to last a lifetime and only a couple of people will ever be that close, your Sacred Trust may shift through the years.

Think of Jesus and his disciples as you imagine these levels of relationship. He seemed to have a deeper relationship with Peter, James, and John than with all the others. These three represent his Inner Circle. When he was hanging on the cross, Jesus asked John to take care of his mother. He invited only Peter, James, and John to be with him in the Garden of Gethsemane. They had something unique between them.

But Jesus still had meaningful relationships with all twelve disciples. The twelve represent his Sacred Trust. The people in your Sacred Trust understand that *we carry each other's burdens*. If it means flying across the country to support my friend, then I am buying the plane ticket. We can't do this for everyone. But we should all seek to build relationships that go this deep. Relationships at this level are more than friends—they are spiritual brothers and sisters deeply and personally committed to one another.

It sounds really spiritual to say that we will treat all people with this level of access. But even Jesus limited his Sacred Trust to twelve people. No matter how much you might want to, you can't have twenty-five people in your Sacred Trust. It's impossible to stay that close with so many.

The fourth level of relationship is **The Family of Faith**. This specifically refers to your local church, and you should of course express a deeper relational commitment to your local congregation. But this circle also includes believers outside your congregation. The nature of this relationship is *spiritual*; you are one body brought together in Jesus. It doesn't mean you always get along or that you always see eye to eye. The defining characteristic of this circle is *shared devotion*. Jesus means everything to all of you, and Scripture teaches that we should go out of our way for those in the Family of Faith (Galatians 6:10).

Sometimes Christians are afraid to develop the first three levels of the relationships outlined above, so we end up putting unrealistic pressure on the entire Family of Faith. We expect every Christian we know to reach out when we are in trouble and every pastor at the church to visit us when we have a need. But pastors are not called to do all the ministry. They are called to equip the saints to do the work of the ministry (Ephesians 4:12). When each member of the church takes responsibility to intentionally develop deep relationships, these *boundaries sustain growth* and the entire body of Christ can thrive.

The fifth level of relationship is **Partnerships**. The defining characteristic of these relationships is that they are *transactional*. Partnerships exist, for example, between business partners, employees and employers, and coaches and athletes. Partnerships do not necessarily need to be between two Christians. The defining characteristic of the Partnership circle is we *depend on one another*. Some relationships will remain at the Partnership level, and there is nothing necessarily wrong with that. Not everyone will move beyond Partnership, and not every relationship needs to.

The outer level of relationship is **The Neighbor**. For the Christian, your neighbor includes every person you come into contact with. It includes the person you meet from a different culture or background. It even includes your enemy (Luke 10:25–37). The nature of this relationship is *practical*. You might open a door for them as you enter a building. You might invite them to go first in the grocery line. The defining characteristic is simply *opportunity*. You find yourself sharing the same space. The Scriptures teach us to do good to all people as we have opportunity (Galatians 6:10).

These six levels of relationship can help clarify our expectations with different people in our lives. We can't be everything to everyone. We can't expect everyone to be everything for us. We shouldn't expect our Inner Circle to provide what only God can provide. We shouldn't expect a Partnership to fill the need that the Family of Faith is called to fill. Reflecting on the different levels of relationship can help eliminate unhealthy pressure and unrealistic expectations. It can also help us focus on growing deeper relationships that might be missing in our lives.

We don't need to categorize every person we know into one of these levels. We don't need to fill each level as though it were a quota. To do so would put an unhealthy pressure and rigidity on our relationships. But we can use this tool to help us become more intentional in our relationships and to "rightly size" our expectations. This can help each level of relationship thrive in ways that were not possible before, because *boundaries sustain growth*.

What level of relationship have you been neglecting? Is there one that doesn't exist at all in your life right now? Where have you asked too much or too little from people in your life?

Sometimes Christians use the excuse of "having good boundaries" as a reason to avoid carrying the burdens of others or getting involved in messy situations. Don't make that mistake. Relationships come with a price, but they also come with an enormous return on investment. Whose burden are you helping to carry right now? Who in your life is helping you carry your burden? Until you can answer these questions, you are missing out on the benefits of healthy boundaries.

There was a time in my life when I lived in a multi-family house with nine other Christians. We had what we called "Cereal Club" almost every night, where people would show up in our living room around 10:00 p.m. with a bowl of Captain Crunch or Cheerios. Then my family moved out of that house, and we moved into a single-family home, where friends bought the houses on either side of our new property. People were in and out of our backyard every day, but we could still close the door and have time for our family. The boundaries were different because Chrisy and I were in a different season of life.

Today, it's different again. Our kids are getting older, and we have a little girl growing up in our house who wasn't born into our family. God knit her in perfectly, and a sweet community is growing among the six of us. We lead a small group in our home. Chrisy and I both meet one on one with a handful of younger Christians.

Every season of life requires unique boundaries, but no matter what season you're in, community should *stretch you*. You should feel the pull of vulnerability and the discomfort of proximity. You should engage in real sacrifice. You should enjoy the fun. And you must be intentional about your boundaries. Build the wall too high, and you will find yourself alone. Don't build the wall at all, and you will find yourself depleted. *Boundaries sustain growth.*

— SACRED STEPS —

As you reflect on the content of this chapter, consider taking the following steps to grow:

1. Review the section on the four pitfalls of healthy boundaries: *selfishness*, *pride*, *codependence*, and *enabling*. In your journal, write

down the ten most significant relationships in your life, and examine each one for these four pitfalls. Once you identify concerns, have conversations with those people in your life where you need to clarify the boundaries.

2. Take the six Relationship Circles outlined in this chapter and fill in each circle with names. Who is in your Sacred Trust? Who is in your Partnership circle? Once each circle is filled in, look for gaps. Where are you missing people? Begin to ask God to bring the people you need into the circles you lack. Review the Relationship Circles until all six are filled in with an appropriate number of healthy relationships.

3. Have a direct conversation with every person whom you would consider to be in your Sacred Trust. Discuss the Relationship Circles with them and ask them how they feel about that type of commitment. Hold each other accountable to carry each other's burdens and not carry each other's cargo.

11

A TRUE FRIEND

"What a friend I've found. Closer than a brother."[78]

Martin Smith

"There are two ways to live the Christian life. You can live it either for the heart of Christ or from the heart of Christ."[79]

Dane C. Ortlund

"Every potential friend can become a better friend if I don't give up. The truth is that most of my friends became friends around some type of disagreement."[80]

John M. Perkins

"Fear not, therefore; you are of more value than many sparrows."

Matthew 10:31

In the gospel of Matthew, we read the story of Jesus sending out his twelve disciples. They were young and naive, and they were tasked with the daunting responsibility of forming the first iteration of the *sacred us*. It would be a different sort of community, born out of agape love and eternal in nature.

The church, the people of God, were never intended to simply be an organization or a corporation. It was always God's purpose for his family to look fundamentally different from every other community on earth. We are a living, breathing body—an eternal family, marked by transcendent friendship.

As Jesus pushed the baby birds out of the nest, he addressed the biggest concern in the hearts of his disciples. They were *afraid*. They were afraid of being persecuted and rejected by the world. They were afraid of failure, and afraid that they didn't know enough. I think they were afraid of the cost that comes with a community like this, both personally and emotionally. And their fear wasn't unfounded. Many of them would suffer the hurt of betrayal, abandonment, and failed friendship. The sacred us would not be perfect. How would the disciples endure?

> We are a living, breathing
> body—an eternal family, marked
> by transcendent friendship.

As we reflect on the seven principles of biblical community outlined in this book, it's natural to feel this same sense of fear. Do you really want to be so close to other Christians that they can see the warts and scars in your life? Wouldn't it be so much easier to just show up on Sunday, pray with a few people, and go about your business? Vulnerability is terrifying. Sacrifice is uncomfortable. When we actually live these principles, they invade the cocoon of our personal space and cause something inside us to want to retreat.

You might read a book like this and think to yourself, *Well, that's nice ... for other people. But I don't think I'm ready to be involved in a community like that.* What makes the sacred us work? How do we learn to endure the failures, forgive one another, and live out biblical community even when it's immature and half-formed?

Jesus addressed his disciples' fears directly. He said, "Do not fear those who kill the body but cannot kill the soul. Rather fear him who can destroy both soul and body in hell. Are not two sparrows sold for a penny? And not one of them will fall to the ground apart from your Father. But even the hairs of your head are all numbered. Fear not, therefore; you are of more value than many sparrows" (Matthew 10:28–31).

His logic can be a bit confusing at first. It seems that he's telling us *to fear* and *not to fear* in the same breath. He was introducing to his disciples the concept of the *fear of the Lord*. This concept is found throughout the Bible and is central to understanding a right relationship to God. To know God is to fear him, but not in the way that you fear a terrifying tyrant. God doesn't want his children to see him that way.

The fear of the Lord carries with it a sense of awe, wonder, and terror, but it's different from horror or dread. It means that you value God so highly that you are terrified of ever being apart from him. You recognize the truth of his glory, and you value him above all others. This is the fear of the Lord. Jesus wants us to know that when we reverence God above all else, our hearts can find a supernatural freedom from every other fear.

Then Jesus started talking about *sparrows*. He tells us that God pays attention to every single one. It seems like a pretty hard left turn, but he was uncovering the layers of fear that existed within his disciples, because stepping into the sacred us can stir up the fear of being overlooked. If you're just one little part of this big, holy community, what if you're forgotten or ignored? What if vulnerability doesn't create connection but instead creates only humiliation? What if mission morphs into obligation and becomes manipulation rather than adventure? What if you sacrifice but no one else does and you're left holding all the responsibility alone?

No one wants to be overlooked, and let's face it—people are *flawed*. They will let you down, turn you down, and sometimes push you down. Even Jesus protected his heart from the fickle inconsistencies of people (John 2:24). How can we form the *sacred us* if all of *us* are guarded and half-committed?

To really grow a healthy biblical community requires that we first understand something about God. We must see that he is more involved than we realize. He's not a clockmaker who set the world in motion and then simply observes from a distance. Rather, God is attentive, active, and central to the growth of a healthy community. God is the one who pays attention to every detail—even the life and death of *every* sparrow.

According to scientists, there are approximately 1.6 billion sparrows on planet Earth and over 50 billion birds worldwide.[81] Somehow God is not too busy to keep track of every single one. Jesus tells us that God even numbers the hairs on your head (Matthew 10:30). Consider the implications of this statement. There are roughly eight billion people in the world, and the average person has around 100,000 hairs.[82] Do the math. That's a lot of hairs to keep track of. Why would Jesus say these things? Was this hyperbole? Was he simply waxing poetic? I don't think so.

Do you remember your first day of kindergarten? I do. I was so excited to go, but at the same time I was terrified to get on the bus and say goodbye to my mom. Everything was different—the sights, the smells, the sounds. But there was one thing that made me feel so much better: my older brother, Russ, was getting on the bus with me. He sat next to me even though it wasn't cool to sit with the little kids and he was two grades older. I wasn't alone.

Jesus wants you to know that he's not asking you to enter into the sacred us alone. In fact, you will never be alone again—not in life, not in death, and not after death. He promises to be with you every step of the way. He will sit with you on the bus. And this is the secret of the sacred us. It is a community centered on Jesus, the one person who will never leave you. When friends fail you, he will not. When people leave, he won't. When death steals your closest relationships, Jesus still remains.

> God is attentive, active, and central to the growth of a healthy community.

Thomas à Kempis wrote, "Love [Jesus], and keep Him for your friend, and He will stand by you when all other friends depart, and will not suffer you to perish at the last. You must one day be severed from all."[83] When that day comes, Jesus will be there.

Some Christians use the faithfulness of Jesus as an excuse to keep other people at arm's length. "All I need is Jesus," they say. But the faithfulness of Jesus should not compel you to distance yourself from others. It should compel you to risk deeper relationship, since your greatest inner stability comes from Christ.

How do we live in such a way that the stability of Jesus deepens all our other relationships? He teaches us how through his story about sparrows.

Consider the Sparrow

"Are not two sparrows sold for a penny? And not one of them will fall to the ground apart from your Father" (Matthew 10:29). Why did Jesus mention *two* sparrows? And who was buying sparrows anyway? The people in that time didn't buy sparrows for pets. They might buy sparrows for food, but that doesn't sound like much of a meal. There was one reason, however, for someone to buy or sell sparrows. Every good Jew in Jesus' time knew that they were sold in Israel for the ritual cleansing of leprosy. According to the Old Testament, the process of cleansing a leper and bringing that person back into community required *two* sparrows (Leviticus 14:4).

Leprosy is a brutal disease. It rots the flesh until it literally falls off the bone. The lepers in Jesus' day lived outside the camp. They weren't allowed to associate with anyone else. They were ostracized and isolated—the epitome of an *outsider*.

Leprosy in the Bible is frequently used as a picture of sin. Allegorically speaking, what leprosy does on the outside, sin does on the inside. As leprosy rots the flesh, so sin rots the soul. As leprosy had no cure at the time, so also sin has no cure if God does not intervene. The leper outside the camp represents our life outside the gospel. We can't come close to God or others because sin keeps us in isolation. Here's how the two sparrows were used in the cleansing of the leper:

> The LORD spoke to Moses, saying, "This shall be the law of the leprous person for the day of his cleansing. He shall be brought to the priest, and the priest shall go out of the camp, and the priest shall look. Then, if the case of leprous disease is healed in the leprous person, the priest shall command them to take for him who is to be cleansed two live clean birds and *cedarwood and scarlet yarn and hyssop*. And the priest shall command them to *kill one* of the birds in an *earthenware vessel* over fresh water. He shall take the live bird with the cedarwood and the scarlet yarn and the hyssop, and *dip them* and the live bird in the *blood* of the bird that was killed over the fresh water. And he shall sprinkle it seven times on him who is to be cleansed of the leprous disease. Then he shall pronounce him clean and shall *let the living bird go* into the open field." (Leviticus 14:1–7)

This sounds like a pretty strange ceremony. Why would God go through all this trouble? Everything in this ritual is there to teach us about God's eternal plan. It's a symbolic road map to understanding his bigger purpose. The cedar and the hyssop carry an important meaning. Cedar was considered the royal wood; it was the wood they used to build the temple. And hyssop was the lowliest of plants.

The phrase "from the cedar to the hyssop" meant that someone went from the highest of highs to the lowest of lows (see 1 Kings 4:33).

The scarlet thread represents blood. God wanted us to know that his entire plan for humanity would be "tied together" with the thread of his blood. The word used for "birds" in this text is the Hebrew word used to describe small birds and is sometimes directly translated "sparrow." The birds represent *you* as you stand before God. Notice that there are two birds, not one, because you don't stand before God alone. The first bird represents Jesus, who will stand with you forever. He is the one who went from the highest place in heaven to the lowest place on the cross—from the cedar to the hyssop. And his blood tied everything together.

Just as the first sparrow was washed with the fresh water, so Christ was washed with the living water of the Spirit. The bird was killed in an earthenware vessel, just as Christ wore the earthenware vessel of a human body.

Remember, the second bird was then dipped in the blood of the bird who had been killed. The first bird's body "falls to the ground," and the second bird is set free. The leper was sprinkled with blood and welcomed back into the community. All of this serves as an illustration to reveal the heart of the gospel and the secret of the *sacred us*.

I can just imagine Jesus, with a twinkle in his eye, looking at his disciples and saying, "The bird who fell to the ground did not do it apart from your father." God had a plan. God knew that we needed a stabilizing force at the center if biblical community was ever going to thrive. And he accounted for every detail, just as he counts the hairs on your head.

Jesus is the first bird, the one who died so that you could be free, and so that the leprosy of your sin could be cleansed. You are the second bird, washed in his blood and set free to fly. You are also the leper who has been healed and approved by the priest. You can now enter community forgiven of all sin and free from all fear.

You can walk into the camp—the sacred us—clean, your confidence no longer rooted in the approval of others but in the ironclad decree of the high priest. And even when other people fail you, and they will, your identity is secure because you know you've been approved by the priest himself.

It was in this context that Jesus told his disciples to *fear not.* Don't fear suffering. Don't fear persecution. Don't fear the challenges of close relationship. God will give you the strength to risk vulnerability and make uncommon sacrifices. He will empower you to love even when people fail you. He will stand with you just as the two birds stood together.

Jesus himself has modeled for us the seven principles of biblical community. He has perfectly performed each one as a living example for us, and through his strength in us, we can find a new capacity to commit ourselves more deeply to community.

Proximity provides opportunity. Jesus led the way by coming as close to us as supernaturally possible. First, he came physically by taking on flesh and blood, and then he came into the Christian's heart through the Holy Spirit. The opportunity for deep community is now possible through him.

Vulnerability creates connection. God became vulnerable in Christ and was fully exposed on the cross. He took our nakedness so that we could take his robe of righteousness, and he did it before we ever chose him. He put himself out there without any reservations so we could learn to put ourselves out there and risk being hurt.

Discipleship sets direction. Jesus modeled the way through a perfect life and taught us that leaders should be the first to serve. He became of no reputation, and God exalted him to the highest position. He was courageous, humble, honest, and kind. He showed us a life of purpose and taught us to live for the upward call.

Fun amplifies grace. Jesus turned water into wine for his first miracle, and he was playful with the disciples on the beach after his resurrection. He is the God who is eternally happy, and he teaches our hearts to celebrate his grace no matter what we face in life.

Mission drives adventure. Jesus ripped the keys of death out of Satan's hands, then revealed to us his great eternal mission: *making all things new.* He invited us to participate in the mission by entrusting his people with the gospel. As we follow his example and give ourselves for others, we discover the greatest adventure this life has to offer.

Sacrifice matures love. Jesus made the ultimate sacrifice, not because he had to but because he chose to. He showed us a higher love and revealed to us the heart of God. His love compels us beyond ourselves into a life of sacrifice for others.

Boundaries sustain growth. Jesus lived submitted to the limits imposed by God, and this empowered his life to reshape eternity. Still, he will never do for us what we must do for ourselves. He will carry our burdens with us, but he expects us to carry our cargo. He creates limits for our good, and as we trust his limits, we learn to thrive.

If you take these seven principles of biblical community and apply them in your life, at times you will be hurt, exposed, overlooked, or offended—but you will not be alone. *Not ever.* God will reveal himself to you, and he will knit your heart with his. He will use your life to form the *sacred us* and enable you to build friendships that transcend anything this world has to offer.

You will see his mission advance in ways that are impossible on your own. And you will find a new *joy*—the joy that comes when agape love stretches your heart wider and wider. Jesus is the true friend, and he leads us into true friendship. You don't have to be afraid of the cost. He has gone ahead of you, and he has already told us that it will be worth it. *Behold, I am with you always.*

Onward

The *sacred us*. In my heart, those words ring with a sort of awe and wonder. What is it really? It's that *thing* you know you need but that the church so often lacks. It's more than friendship, more than buddies. It's more than a night out with the guys or getting together with old friends. It's even more than family.

The sacred us is the transcendent community knit together by the Spirit of Jesus, bound more deeply to Christ and one another than any natural relationship in life. It's the great dance—the divine collision of intimacy with God, knowledge of self, and connection to others.

The sacred us is perfect and yet at the same time in process. It's perfect because Christ is at the center and his cross makes us right with God. His grace gives us supernatural power to reconcile with others. But living the sacred us is messy, clumsy, offensive, and inconvenient. It comes with a host of challenges, but it also serves as the doorway to greater joy and the training ground for a higher love.

Will you risk vulnerability? Will you intentionally go deeper with others? The world waits for a community ruled by love. Maybe your little group can serve as a spark of light that spreads further than you ever imagined.

— SACRED STEPS —

As you come to the end of *The Sacred Us*, consider taking the following steps to grow:

1. If you haven't already, read this book with a group of five to ten other Christians, and meet to discuss each chapter together. Apply the "Sacred Steps" at the end of each chapter, and hold one another accountable to grow.

2. Use the Sacred Us Assessment Tool to explore the strengths and weaknesses of your personal community. Map out a plan to strengthen the areas in your life that are weak.

3. Within your small group or sacred trust, make a commitment to no longer accept "church as usual." Begin a movement at your church with the help of your leaders to revive intentional community across your church. Practice the seven principles together until they help form a new culture of deeper relationships.

THE SACRED US ASSESSMENT TOOL

Healthy community grows only through intentionality. This assessment tool will help you identify the principles of community that need attention in your life. On a scale of 1 to 10, with 1 being "never true of me" and 10 being "always true of me," rate where you fall in each area. After you have filled in your answers, circle any scores below 6. If you have more than one score below 6 in a category, make that principle the focus of your growth.

1. Proximity Provides Opportunity

I am present and engaged when talking with others.

1   2   3   4   5   6   7   8   9   10

I spend large amounts of my free time connecting with others.

1   2   3   4   5   6   7   8   9   10

My life is deeply impacted by the regular physical nearness of other Christians.

1   2   3   4   5   6   7   8   9   10

I have a small group of people in my life whom I would drive across the country to support.

1   2   3   4   5   6   7   8   9   10

2. Vulnerability Creates Connection

I do not regularly battle with shame.

1   2   3   4   5   6   7   8   9   10

I have found consistent victory over the impostor syndrome.

1   2   3   4   5   6   7   8   9   10

I am comfortable sharing my hurts, failures, and flaws.

1   2   3   4   5   6   7   8   9   10

I open my heart quickly to others.

1   2   3   4   5   6   7   8   9   10

3. Discipleship Sets Direction

I live with a deep sense of the upward call of God guiding my life.

1   2   3   4   5   6   7   8   9   10

I have personally committed every aspect of my life to Jesus.

1   2   3   4   5   6   7   8   9   10

I have other Christians in my life who regularly challenge me in my spiritual growth.

1   2   3   4   5   6   7   8   9   10

I am willing and comfortable confronting others in a gracious and direct way when needed.

1   2   3   4   5   6   7   8   9   10

4. Fun Amplifies Grace

I laugh often because I understand that fun is a biblical idea.

1   2   3   4   5   6   7   8   9   10

I see God as gloriously happy within himself.

1   2   3   4   5   6   7   8   9   10

I regularly have a lot of fun with Christian friends.

1   2   3   4   5   6   7   8   9   10

I don't dishonor or belittle others for the sake of a laugh.

1   2   3   4   5   6   7   8   9   10

5. Mission Drives Adventure

My life is lived with a sense of God-given adventure.

1   2   3   4   5   6   7   8   9   10

I am deeply passionate and excited about other people meeting Jesus.

1   2   3   4   5   6   7   8   9   10

In the past few months, I can think of many adventures I've had with other Christians.

1   2   3   4   5   6   7   8   9   10

God often uses me to bring his life and peace into a dead situation.

1   2   3   4   5   6   7   8   9   10

6. Sacrifice Matures Love

I have recognized my tendency toward a selfish and barren heart and have seen incredible growth.

1   2   3   4   5   6   7   8   9   10

The love of God fuels my desire to sacrifice for others.

1   2   3   4   5   6   7   8   9   10

I have joyfully made significant sacrifices for others in the last three to six months.

1   2   3   4   5   6   7   8   9   10

I can see the depth of my love for God and others growing year over year.

1   2   3   4   5   6   7   8   9   10

7. Boundaries Sustain Growth

I have healthy boundaries in my relationships.

1   2   3   4   5   6   7   8   9   10

I know what my "cargo" is, and I don't ask others to carry it for me.

1   2   3   4   5   6   7   8   9   10

I can think of times in the last three months when I helped carry someone else's burden.

1   2   3   4   5   6   7   8   9   10

I have thought through the six Relationship Circles, and each one is healthy in my life.

1   2   3   4   5   6   7   8   9   10

NOTES

1. C. S. Lewis, *They Stand Together: The Letters of C. S. Lewis to Arthur Greeves, 1914–1963* (London: Collins, 1979), 477.

2. Frederick Buechner, *Secrets in the Dark: A Life in Sermons* (San Francisco: HarperSanFrancisco, 2007), 300.

3. Joan Powers, inspired by A. A. Milne, *Pooh's Little Instruction Book* (New York: Dutton Books, 1995).

4. Pete D'Amato, "How Did a Middle Class Woman with Nine Siblings Lie Dead and Unnoticed for Five Years? Tragic Story of Michigan IT Worker, 44, Found Mummified When Her Home Was Seized over Unpaid Bills," *Daily Mail*, March 5, 2015, www.dailymail.co.uk/news/article-2974499/How-Michigan -woman-nine-siblings-end-mummified-backseat-car-remain-five-years.html.

5. Robert D. Putnam, *Bowling Alone: The Collapse and Revival of American Community* (New York: Simon & Schuster, 2000), 183, 287.

6. "Loneliness and the Workplace: 2020 U.S. Report," Cigna, www.cigna .com/static/www-cigna-com/docs/about-us/newsroom/studies-and-reports /combatting-loneliness/cigna-2020-loneliness-report.pdf, 2.

7. Stephen Marche, "Is Facebook Making Us Lonely?" *The Atlantic*, May 2012, www.theatlantic.com/magazine/archive/2012/05/is-facebook-making-us-lonely /308930/.

8. Ross Douthat, "The Age of Individualism," *New York Times*, March 15, 2014, www.nytimes.com/2014/03/16/opinion/sunday/douthat-the-age-of-individualism .html.

9. J. C. Ryle, *Practical Religion Unabridged* (London: William Hunt, 1880), 209.

10. J. R. R. Tolkien, *The Lord of the Rings: The Return of the King* (New York: Del Rey Books, 2018), 241.

11. Tony Evans, *One Church under God: His Rule over Your Ministry* (Chicago: Moody, 2014), 76.

12. Maya Angelou (@DrMayaAngelou), Twitter, July 13, 2015, 2:03 p.m., https:// twitter.com/drmayaangelou/status/620654782273880064?lang=en.

13. Brené Brown, *The Gifts of Imperfection: Let Go of Who You Think You're Supposed to Be and Embrace Who You Are* (Center City, MN: Hazelden, 2010), 26.

14. John Piper, "Can We Explain the Trinity?" *Desiring God*, March 30, 2020, www.desiringgod.org/articles/can-we-explain-the-trinity.

15. Cornelius Plantinga Jr., *Engaging God's World: A Christian Vision of Faith, Learning, and Living* (Grand Rapids, MI: Eerdmans, 2002), 20–21, 23.

16. C. S. Lewis, *Mere Christianity* (New York: HarperCollins, 2001), 175.

17. Augustine, *Confessions*, trans. Rex Warner (New York: Mentor, 1963).

18. Timothy Keller, *Jesus the King: Understanding the Life and Death of the Son of God* (New York: Penguin, 2016), 10–11.

19. *Gladiator*, directed by Ridley Scott (Universal City, CA: DreamWorks Pictures, 2000).

20. Timothy Keller, "Connecting People to One Another," ch. 24 in *Center Church: Doing Balanced, Gospel-Centered Ministry in Your Community* (Grand Rapids, MI: Zondervan, 2012).

21. Rick Warren, *The Purpose Driven Life: What on Earth Am I Here For?* exp. ed. (Grand Rapids, MI: Zondervan, 2012), 138.

22. Leonard Ravenhill, *Why Revival Tarries* (Minneapolis, MN: Bethany House, 1987), 71.

23. Dietrich Bonhoeffer, *Life Together: The Classic Exploration of Christian Community* (New York: HarperCollins, 1954), 19.

24. The Jackson 5, "I'll Be There," by Berry Gordy, Hal Davis, Bob West, and Willie Hutch, track 1 on *Third Album*, Motown Records, 1970.

25. David Benner, *The Gift of Being Yourself: The Sacred Call to Self Discovery* (Downers Grove, IL: IVP Books, 2015), 49.

26. James Taylor, "You've Got a Friend," by Carole King, track 2 on *Mud Slide Slim and the Blue Horizon*, Warner Bros. Records, 1971.

27. Frederick Buechner, *The Clown in the Belfry: Writings on Faith and Fiction* (San Francisco: HarperSanFrancisco, 1992), 156–57.

28. Allan and Barbara Pease, "The Definitive Book of Body Language," *New York Times*, September 24, 2006, www.nytimes.com/2006/09/24/books/chapters /0924-1st-peas.html.

29. Henri J. M. Nouwen, *The Genesee Diary: Report from a Trappist Monastery* (New York: Doubleday, 1976), 56.

30. C. S. Lewis, *The Four Loves* (New York: Harcourt, Brace, 1960).

31. Timothy Keller, "The Gifts of Christmas," ch. 5 in *Come, Thou Long-Expected Jesus: Experiencing the Peace and Promise of Christmas*, ed. Nancy Guthrie (Wheaton, IL: Crossway Books, 2008), 38.

32. John Stott, *The Cross: Thirteen Studies for Individuals or Groups* (Downers Grove, IL: InterVarsity, 2009), 55.

33. George Bernard Shaw, *Man and Superman: A Comedy and a Philosophy* (Cambridge: The University Press, 1905), 13.

34. Carl Jung, quoted in Ross Rosenberg, "Unearthing and Ridding Yourself of Toxic Shame," Psych Central, November 13, 2013, https://psychcentral.com/blog /unearthing-ridding-yourself-of-toxic-shame#1.

35. Ernest Hemingway, *The Old Man and the Sea* (Beirut, Lebanon: World Heritage, 2015), 65.

36. Judith Shulevitz, "Bring Back the Sabbath," *New York Times Magazine*, March 2, 2003, www.nytimes.com/2003/03/02/magazine/bring-back-the-sabbath.html.

37. Lewis, *Four Loves*, 169–70.

38. Gene Edwards, *A Tale of Three Kings: A Study in Brokenness*, 2nd ed. (Carol Stream, IL: Tyndale, 1992), ch. 3.

39. Philip Yancey, *What's So Amazing About Grace?* (Grand Rapids, MI: Zondervan, 1997), 55.

40. Tony Evans, "Grace is all that God has done *for* you, independent *of* you," Facebook, March 10, 2015, www.facebook.com/drtonyevans.

41. Timothy Keller and Kathy Keller, *The Meaning of Marriage: Facing the Complexities of Commitment with the Wisdom of God* (New York: Riverhead Books, 2011), 101.

42. John F. Kennedy, speech, Raleigh, NC, September 17, 1960, www.jfklibrary .org/archives/other-resources/john-f-kennedy-speeches/raleigh-nc-19600917.

43. Henry Cloud, *Necessary Endings: The Employees, Businesses, and Relationships That All of Us Have to Give Up in Order to Move Forward* (New York: HarperCollins, 2010), 106–7.

44. Chris Widener, *Jim Rohn's Eight Best Success Lessons* (Issaquah, WA: Made for Success, 2014), lesson 6.

45. Buzz Aldrin and Wayne Warga, *Return to Earth* (New York: Open Road Media, 2015).

46. Leo Tolstoy, *Confession*, trans. David Patterson (New York: W. W. Norton, 1996), 30, 35–36, 92, emphasis added.

47. Lewis, *Mere Christianity*, 136–37.

48. M. Robert Mulholland Jr., *Invitation to a Journey: A Road Map for Spiritual Formation* (Downers Grove, IL: InterVarsity, 2016), 51.

49. Martin Luther, quoted in *The Westminster Collection of Christian Quotes: Over 6,000 Quotes Arranged by Theme*, comp. Martin H. Manser (Louisville, KY: Westminster John Knox, 2001), 225.

50. Pharrell Williams, "Happy," track 5 on *Girl*, Columbia, 2014.

51. Charles Spurgeon, Susannah Spurgeon, and W. J. Harrald, *The Autobiography of Charles H. Spurgeon*, vol. 3, 1856–1878 (Chicago: Fleming H. Revell, 1899), 339.

52. Lawrence Robinson, Melinda Smith, and Jeanne Segal, "Laughter Is the Best Medicine," HelpGuide, July 2021, www.helpguide.org/articles/mental-health /laughter-is-the-best-medicine.htm.

53. David Cameron, "Having Happy Friends Can Make You Happy," *Harvard Gazette*, December 5, 2008, https://news.harvard.edu/gazette/story/2008/12 /having-happy-friends-can-make-you-happy/. See also James H. Fowler and Nicholas A. Christakis, "Dynamic Spread of Happiness in a Large Social Network: Longitudinal Analysis over 20 Years in the Framingham Heart Study," *BMJ*, December 5, 2008, www.bmj.com/content/337/bmj.a2338.full.

54. Jonathan Edwards, "A Dissertation Concerning the End for Which God Created the World," Monergism, accessed February 21, 2022, www.monergism .com/dissertation-concerning-end-which-god-created-world-jonathan-edwards.

55. Frederick Buechner, "Laughter of Biblical Proportions," Renovaré, January 2000, https://renovare.org/articles/laughter-of-biblical-proportions.

56. Frederick Buechner, *Telling the Truth: The Gospel as Tragedy, Comedy, and Fairy Tale* (San Francisco: HarperSanFrancisco, 1977), 66.

57. C. S. Lewis, *The Weight of Glory: And Other Addresses* (New York: HarperCollins, 2001), 46.

58. Martin Luther King Jr., "Keep Moving from This Mountain," speech, Spelman College, Atlanta, GA, April 10, 1960. See Martin Luther King Jr. Research and Education Institute, accessed February 21, 2022, https://kinginstitute.stanford .edu/king-papers/documents/keep-moving-mountain-address-spelman-college-10 -april-1960.

59. Bill Bright, *The Joy of Trusting God: Character You Can Count On* (Colorado Springs: David C Cook, 2005), 14.

60. Bo Jackson and Dick Schaap, *Bo Knows Bo: The Autobiography of a Ballplayer* (New York: Doubleday, 1990), 200.

61. "Walt's Quotes," D23 Official Disney Fan Club, accessed February 21, 2022, https://d23.com/section/walt-disney-archives/walts-quotes/.

62. "Others," Salvation Army Metro Phoenix, accessed February 21, 2022, www.salvationarmyphoenix.org/copy-of-about-us.

63. *To Love This Life: Quotations by Helen Keller* (New York: AFB, 2000), 35.

64. N. D. Wilson, "The Dark-Tinted, Truth-Filled Reading List We Owe Our Kids," *Christianity Today*, January 8, 2014, www.christianitytoday.com/ct/2014 /january-february/dark-tinted-truth-filled-reading-list-our-kids-need.html.

65. H. Jackson Brown Jr., comp., *P.S. I Love You* (Nashville, TN: Rutledge Hill, 1990), 13.

66. "Higher Love," by Steve Winwood and Will Jennings, track 1 on *Back in the High Life*, Island Records, 1986.

67. Elisabeth Elliot, *Marriage: A Revolution and a Revelation*, Internet Archive, 2010, accessed February 22, 2022, https://tinyurl.com/ycnw3ecn, p. 13.

68. Henri Nouwen, "Community, a Quality of the Heart," Henri Nouwen Society, January 23, 2018, https://henrinouwen.org/meditation/community-a-quality -of-the-heart/.

69. Richard Wurmbrand, *Tortured for Christ: 50th Anniversary Edition* (Colorado Springs: David C Cook, 2017), 75.

70. R. C. Sproul, *The Intimate Marriage: A Practical Guide to Building a Good Marriage* (Phillipsburg, NJ: P&R, 2003), 53.

71. Lewis, *Mere Christianity*, 132.

72. Amy Carmichael, quoted in *Westminster Collection of Christian Quotes*, 122.

73. Gwen Costello, *Spiritual Gems from Mother Teresa* (New London, CT: Twenty-Third Publications, 2008), 11.

74. Henry Cloud and John Townsend, *Boundaries: When to Say Yes, How to Say No to Take Control of Your Life* (Grand Rapids, MI: Zondervan, 1992), 31.

75. Thomas Merton, *No Man Is an Island* (Boston: Shambhala, 2005), 177–78.

76. "I'm Goin' Down" by Bruce Springsteen, track 9 on *Born in the U.S.A.*, Columbia, 1984.

77. Cloud and Townsend, *Boundaries*, 279.

78. Delirious?, "What a Friend I've Found," track 25 on *Deeper: The Definitive Worship Experience*, Integrity Music, 1994.

79. Dane C. Ortlund, *Gentle and Lowly: The Heart of Christ for Sinners and Sufferers* (Wheaton, IL: Crossway, 2020).

80. John M. Perkins, *One Blood: Parting Words to the Church on Race and Love* (Chicago: Moody, 2018), 166.

81. Douglas Main, "How Many Birds Are There in the World?," *National Geographic*, May 17, 2021, www.nationalgeographic.com/animals/article/how -many-birds-are-there-in-the-world-science-estimates#:~:text=Many%20 sparrows%2C%20few%20rarities,a%20population%20of%201.6%20billion.

82. Jill Seladi-Schulman, "How Many Hairs Are on the Human Head?," Healthline, September 30, 2019, www.healthline.com/health/how-many-hairs-on-a-human-head.

83. Thomas à Kempis, *Of the Imitation of Christ* (London: Rivingtons, 1875), 82–83.

ABOUT THE AUTHOR

Justin Kendrick is the lead pastor of Vox Church, which he founded in 2011 with a group of friends on the doorstep of Yale University. Since then, the church has grown to multiple locations across New England with the dream of seeing the least churched region of the US become the most spiritually vibrant place on earth. In addition to *The Sacred Us*, Justin is the author of *Bury Your Ordinary: Practical Habits of a Heart Fully Alive* (David C Cook, 2021). He continues to create sermon material, small group studies, and video content weekly through Vox Church. Justin and his wife, Chrisy, live with their four children in the New Haven area.

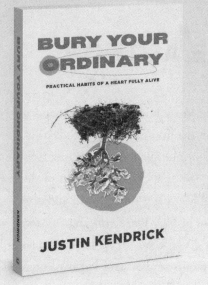

MORE by JUSTIN KENDRICK

Bury Your Ordinary is a field manual to an entirely different way of life in which you dig a deep hole, put the "ordinary you" inside it, cover it with dirt, and walk away as a new person—the real you.

Through intentional changes to your habits, you will discover a deeper love for God and a deeper understanding of yourself. Be challenged to stretch beyond your comfort zones as you discover:

- Seven habits that lead to explosive spiritual growth
- The one change to your routine that will give you an entirely new way of living
- How our routines can either free us or keep us bound
- The key ingredient God looks for in a disciple-maker
- Why God is already deeply satisfied with who you are

For more, including free small group resources, visit **buryyourordinary.com**

 Scan to read the first chapter free!

Available in print, digital, and audio wherever books are sold